seekingthingsabove

A STUDY IN COLOSSIANS

seekingthingsabove

steve pettit

journey**forth**®

Greenville, South Carolina

The fact that materials produced by other publishers may be referred to in this volume does not constitute an endorsement of the content or theological position of materials produced by such publishers.

All Scripture is quoted from the King James Version. Italics indicate the author's emphasis.

Photo Credit: Steve Pettit © 2014, Hal Cook, BJU Photo Services

Seeking Things Above: A Study in Colossians
Steve Pettit

Contributor: Eric Newton
Art Director: Elly Kalagayan
Designer: NaEun Hyun
Page Layout: by Michael Boone

© 2016 BJU Press
Greenville, South Carolina 29614
JourneyForth Books is a division of BJU Press.

Printed in the United States of America
All rights reserved

ISBN 978-1-62856-058-9
eISBN 978-1-62856-279-8

15 14 13 12 11 10 9 8 7 6 5 4 3 2 1

CONTENTS

01

AN INTRODUCTION TO PAUL'S LETTER TO THE COLOSSIANS

Can you think of a time when you introduced yourself to someone for the first time? Perhaps it was a relative at a family reunion or a prospective employer or the parents of a special friend. How about a group of Christians in another country for whom you had been praying? If you had only one opportunity, what would you be sure to say? How would you try to encourage and inspire them? The book of Colossians gives us Paul's answer to these questions.

The Setting

Colossae was located in Phrygia, a region in western Asia Minor (now Turkey). In the centuries before Jesus' birth, the city had been an important, well-populated stop on the trade route from Ephesus to the Euphrates. Colossae was known for its textile industry, particularly a deep red wool.[1] However,

---

[1]Douglas J. Moo, *The Letters to the Colossians and to Philemon*, The Pillar New Testament Commentary (Grand Rapids, Mi.: Eerdmans, 2008), 26.

by the time Paul wrote to the Colossian church in the early 60s, the city was declining and was overshadowed by nearby Laodicea and Hierapolis.[2] In fact, around that same time, an earthquake devastated the region, and Colossae apparently never recovered.

THE PROBLEMS THAT PAUL ADDRESSES IN THIS LETTER INDICATE THAT A SIMILAR MIXTURE OF RELIGIOUS BELIEFS HAD FOUND ITS WAY INTO THE CHURCH.

What makes this epistle distinct from Paul's other letters is that the apostle evidently had not personally established the church at Colossae. These Christians had "not seen [Paul's] face in the flesh" (2:1). Instead, they had heard the gospel through the faithful ministry of Epaphras, Paul's colleague (1:7–8). He was from Colossae—"who is one of you"—(4:12) and had probably been converted during Paul's ministry in Ephesus, 110 miles west of his hometown (Acts 19:10). Paul confirms Epaphras's credibility by announcing that his message was the same gospel being blessed by God throughout the whole world (1:5–6). After pastoring the Colossian church for several years, Epaphras journeyed to Rome in order to update Paul about the condition of the churches of the Lycus Valley (Colossae, Hierapolis, Laodicea) and secure Paul's direction about the errant teaching that had infiltrated the Colossian church. We learn in Philemon that, while in Rome, Epaphras became Paul's "fellowprisoner" (1:23), which meant that Tychicus returned with the letter to the Colossians instead of Epaphras (Col. 4:7).

---

[2]P. T. O'Brien, "Colossians, Letter to the," *Dictionary of Paul and His Letters*, ed. Gerald F. Hawthorne and Ralph P. Martin (Downers Grove: InterVarsity Press, 1993), 147.

The Colossian church consisted primarily of Gentile converts (1:27), which is to be expected. However, Jewish instruction had existed in Colossae through synagogues. Because this town had been a trade center where commodities and ideas were exchanged constantly for centuries, the Judaism taught in these synagogues was not as pure as in Jerusalem. The problems that Paul addresses in this letter indicate that a similar mixture of religious beliefs (often called *syncretism*) had found its way into the church. As one commentator puts it,

> The synagogues had a reputation for laxity and openness to speculation drifting in from the Hellenistic world. In the Colossian church we appear to be in touch with a meeting-place where the free-thinking Judaism of the dispersion and the speculative ideas of Greek mystery-religion are in close contact.[3]

How did the Colossians first receive the gospel? What does this tell us about the ministry of Paul?

_____

_____

_____

_____

_____

[3]Ralph Martin, *Colossians and Philemon*, New Century Bible, ed. Ronald E. Clements and Matthew Black (London: Marshal, Morgan, and Scott, 1974), 18–19.

—personal question   —group question

SEEKING THINGS ABOVE: A STUDY IN COLOSSIANS

The Author

Paul wrote this letter while under house arrest during his first imprisonment in Rome. During this time, he also wrote the other Prison Epistles—Ephesians, Philippians, and Philemon. The purpose of his imprisonment is clear. He asks the Colossians to pray that God would open doors "to speak the mystery of Christ [i.e., the gospel], for which I am also in bonds" (Col. 4:3). Although this particular letter does not indicate whether or not he expects to be freed, we know from Philippians that Paul is hopeful (Phil. 1:25).

Whether imprisoned for Christ's sake or being released to continue His mission, Paul exalts Christ as the center of his life and ministry. He was persuaded that "Christ, . . . is our life" (Col. 3:4), and this conviction permeates his letter to the Colossians. It did not matter that he was incarcerated or that he had never met these believers or that they already knew the gospel and had become converts. He had an opportunity to share his heart, and that meant exalting Christ.

The Situation

What did Paul think was important enough to include in this letter back to Epaphras's congregation? He does not indicate his purpose for writing until the beginning of the second chapter, where he unveils a dual concern: that believers whom he has never met would grow in their knowledge of Christ, and that they would recognize and refuse the heresy that had infiltrated their ranks (2:1–5). Fortunately, this was no full-blown heresy. Paul gives approval and affirmation throughout the epistle. He calls them "saints and faithful brethren in Christ" (1:2). He thanks God for their faith in Christ and love "to all the saints" (1:4) "in the Spirit" (1:8). They unquestionably "knew the grace of God in truth" for the gospel had "[brought] forth fruit" (1:6) among them, just as it was doing in the rest of the inhabited world. Paul even observes their "order, and the stedfastness of [their] faith in Christ" (2:5). But in spite of their seemingly vibrant and solid faith, the Colossians faced significant danger.

What was so dangerous? Though opinions abound concerning the heresy in Colossae, it seems to have involved both pagan and Jewish aspects. What were its characteristics? First, Paul mentions spiritual rulers and authorities several times (1:16; 2:8, 10, 15, 20). These are the evil powers over whom Christ triumphed on the cross (2:15). Paul refers to them as "the rudiments [or elemental spirits] of the world" (2:8), thereby indicating that they rule among the physical domain of this world, not in the presence of God. The temptation was to fear such spirits and seek to appease them through mystic and ascetic practices (2:18, 20–21).

Second, Paul frequently mentions the Creator and creation (1:16–17, 23; 3:10). What problem does this expose? On one hand, the false teachers advocated asceticism by which man can distance himself from the polluted world and, therefore, progress spiritually (2:18, 23). On the other hand, angelic spirits were seen not only as intermediaries but also as authoritative agents of creation, perhaps on par with Christ. If angels enabled access into God's presence, gaining the angels' favor would be vital to successful religion.

A third element of the errant Colossian teaching was reliance on philosophical reasoning and human tradition (2:8, 18, 21–23). Although there is such a things as good tradition, in this context, Paul directly contrasts the term *tradition* with Christ (2:8). The heresy had the appearance of *wisdom* but was humanly-concocted instead of being ordinances received from God (1 Cor. 11:2).

Fourth, some Jewish practices had been identified as crucial to sanctification—"in meat, or in drink, or in respect of an holyday, or of the new moon, or of the sabbath days" (Col. 2:16).

This was not the first church Paul had to warn about the error of relying on external practices (works) instead of faith alone (see Gal. 5:1).

A fifth problem involved a contradictory and unbiblical response to fleshly desires. On one hand, the false teachers pressured the people to observe earthly regulations concerning items not to be touched or eaten (Col. 2:20–21). This physical severity, however, failed to prevent "the satisfying of the flesh" (2:23). In fact, the false sense of spiritual fullness that was derived from these practices probably fostered license among some (3:5–8). They had an external "form of godliness" but their experience was actually "denying the power thereof" (2 Tim. 3:5).

Overall, the false theology encouraged Colossian believers to seek satisfaction in and swear allegiance to intermediary powers and practices. The desire to experience fullness resulted in additions to the gospel—doctrines and practices they thought would supply an entrance into more knowledge and an elevated status. The promise of immediate spiritual satisfaction seemed superior to steady growth in Christ alone.

Someone in the Colossian church had introduced syncretism—the mixture of Christian beliefs with pagan and Jewish practices. What are some examples of syncretism in the twenty-first century? Why are they dangerous?

_____

_____

_____

_____

_____

▌▌ *In what ways do we sometimes attempt to stop our flesh with manmade regulations? Why do we do this even when we know good theology? Why are these attempts futile?*

_____

_____

_____

_____

_____

The Message

In response to this multi-faceted error Paul unequivocally proclaims: "Ye are complete in Him" (Col. 2:10). You can see the centrality of Christ in this epistle merely by scanning its pages. References to Christ occur approximately sixty-five times in its ninety-five verses. The letter evidences its Christological focus in each major section. In his greeting, Paul calls himself "an apostle of *Jesus Christ*" and refers to the Colossians as "faithful brethren in *Christ*" (1:1–2). He gives thanks for their "faith in *Christ Jesus*" (1:4) and shares his prayer for their spiritual maturity in *Christ* (1:9–14). His hymn declares *Christ's* supremacy over both Creation and the church (1:15–23). In Paul's own mission, *Christ* is the message, the goal of Christian maturity, and the enabling strength by which Paul ministers (1:24–2:5). *Christ* is the source of Christian growth (2:6–7) and the antidote for false religion (2:8–23). Paul specifically applies his response to the Colossian problem by explaining that fullness and maturity in *Christ* lead to eternally-focused living (3:1–4:1).

Christ is not just the dominant topic of this Pauline epistle; He is the heart of Paul's message. The Colossians craved the inside track, and Paul had it: "Christ in you, the hope of glory"

(1:27). What these Christians needed was not angelic mediation, Mosaic customs, or monkish abstinence from God's good gifts. All believers, whether first century Colossians or twenty-first century Americans, possess Christ. This is "the mystery which hath been hid from ages and from generations, but now is made manifest to [God's] saints" (1:26). We are privy to "all the treasures of wisdom and knowledge" (2:3) simply by being *in Christ*. Christ powerfully worked in Paul to proclaim his Lord so that he and his missionary team might "present every man perfect in Christ" (1:28).

CHRIST IS NOT JUST THE DOMINANT TOPIC OF THIS PAULINE EPISTLE; HE IS THE HEART OF PAUL'S MESSAGE.

To counter the syncretistic theology that had crept in, Paul declares that Christ alone is supreme and sufficient. All necessary knowledge, fullness, authority, revelation, and salvation dwell in the resurrected Christ, who indwells His people (see Rom. 8:10). Twenty centuries have passed since Paul wrote this letter, but the necessity of focusing on Christ has not. In fact, it is so important that our next chapter is a more in-depth look at what Colossians teaches about Christ.

What is the difference between being "subject to ordinances" in a way that adds to the gospel and a way that properly honors our authorities?

Paul's commitment to the gospel was so strong that it landed him in prison. What can you point to that indicates your own commitment to the gospel? What steps of growth could you pursue?

_____

_____

_____

_____

_____

What did the heresy in Colossae teach about angels? Can you think of any modern parallels to this belief?

_____

_____

_____

_____

Are you tempted to seek immediate spiritual satisfaction? If so, in what ways?

_____

_____

_____

_____

NOTES

02

CHRIST IN COLOSSIANS

COLOSSIANS 2:6–7
As ye have therefore received Christ Jesus the Lord, so walk ye in
him: rooted and built up in him, and stablished in the faith, as ye
have been taught, abounding therein with thanksgiving.

No New Testament letter more specifically or majestically
focuses on Jesus Christ than does Colossians. Like the
threads of an exquisite tapestry, the truths of Christ are woven
together to form this letter's message. Far from being outdated
language or dead orthodoxy, Paul's emphasis on Christ addresses a tendency that has plagued the church since the first
century: the error of relegating the Lord to the periphery in
favor of religious effort, cultural acclimation, and contemporary philosophy. In this epistle Paul asserts the exclusivity and
sufficiency of our sovereign Christ. Do we want to persevere
and grow in our faith? Understanding and applying the apostolic teaching about Jesus Christ is essential to doing so. We
will trace two primary themes in Colossians: Christ's supreme
status and Christ's sufficient ministry.

The Supreme Status of Christ

Many people today profess to be *naturalists*. In other words,
they believe that what we see and taste and smell and hear and

touch and study in a science lab is all there is. Supernatural realities like God and the human soul are denied by definition. However, even though the world has supposedly moved past the need to believe in the supernatural, there is ongoing fascination with superhuman beings and extraterrestrial places. Kids aren't the only ones who watch movies about galactic warfare and superheroes and powerful wizards. Even in our highly technical scientific society, there is something mysteriously compelling about what might surpass the natural world. We long for transcendence. We are very much like first-century Colossians.

Christ Is Lord of Creation

COLOSSIANS 1:16–17

For by him were all things created, that are in heaven, and that are in earth, visible and invisible, whether they be thrones, or dominions, or principalities, or powers: all things were created by him, and for him. And he is before all things, and by him all things consist.

The false teacher in the Colossian church was evidently promoting the importance of cosmic beings. Paul counters the supposed importance of angelic and demonic powers by asserting in Colossians 1 that Christ is Lord over the universe and head of the church. The apostle punctuates the universality of Christ's supremacy with repeated references to *every* and *all* (eight times in Col. 1:15–20). God created "all things" by Christ, who is "before all things" and holds together "all things" and deserves preeminence in "all things" and is the means of reconciliation of "all things" to God. The Holy Spirit could hardly be more inclusive and dogmatic. The term *image* portrays Christ as the pre-existent revelation of God. His divine identity is not derived as Adam's was. He is not simply *made* in God's image; He *is* God's image. And because of that, He rules over all!

Furthermore, we see Christ's preeminence over creation as both the agent of its existence and the reason for its existence (1:16). Christ preceded all created things in time because He is the eternal God—"before all things" (1:17). In the book of Genesis, Moses announced that all of creation finds its origin in a supernatural creator God (Gen. 1:1). The Old Testament reveals the name of this Creator as Jehovah. Jehovah means "the self-existing One" or the great "I AM." That is, God is a self-sufficient being and depends on no one for His existence. Since God is the only self-sufficient One, every created thing is totally dependent on Him. When Paul portrays Jesus Christ as the Creator, he is simultaneously declaring that Jesus is Jehovah of the Old Testament. In John 8:58, Jesus made a self-proclamation to the Jews: "Verily, verily, I say unto you, Before Abraham was, I am." Christ is the One by whom all things are made, whether it is physical or spiritual, visible or invisible, human or angelic. Everything finds its source in Jesus Christ.

THE VERY OPPONENTS OF THE MESSIAH OWE THEIR EXISTENCE AND BREATH TO HIS CREATIVE, PROVIDENTIAL POWER.

Christ doubly surpasses angelic powers, according to Paul, since God created the spiritual rulers through Christ, and Christ dethroned them by His atoning victory (Col. 2:15). But His superiority is not merely temporal, as if He had a head start but is now just one of many heavenly beings. He is the chosen Son, the "Firstborn," indicating His loftier rank as appointed Heir and Ruler.[1] (The term *firstborn* does not mean that He was born first but that He holds a superior position above all creation.) In addition, He

---

[1]Thomas R. Schreiner, *Paul, Apostle of God's Glory in Christ: A Pauline Mission* (Downers Grove: InterVarsity Press, 2001), 175–6.

continually upholds creation with His powerful word (Heb. 1:3). God has never been a distant clock-winder, and Christ demonstrates God's immanent involvement in creation by ensuring that "all things consist" (Col. 1:17), which means *hold together*. The very opponents of the Messiah owe their existence and breath to His creative, providential power. In relation to God, Christ is "image;" in relation to the world, He is "firstborn" (1:15).[2]

Christ Is Lord of the New Creation

COLOSSIANS 1:18

And he is the head of the body, the church: who is the beginning, the firstborn from the dead; that in all things he might have the preeminence.

Christ is Lord over not only creation generally but the church, the new creation, specifically. As head of the body, Christ acts as authority over its life. He is the "firstborn from the dead" (1:18), the one who deserves preeminence as "the Founder of a new humanity" (1:18).[3] This new humanity could not have come into existence without the reconciling work of Christ. His preeminence in everything related to salvation stems from His undeniable deity—"it pleased the Father that in him should all fulness dwell" (1:19)—, and from His impeccable humanity. Reconciliation required "the blood of his cross" (1:20), which He gave through "the body of his flesh" (1:22). According to Colossians 1, Christ is Lord over all primarily because He possesses power over life. He creates and sustains. He gave up His own life to ensure the eternal life of all those who "continue in the faith" (1:23). As Lord of heaven and earth

[2]O'Brien, 44.
[3]O'Brien, 50.

and His people forever, Christ (not the angels) deserves our complete submission.

> **Colossians 1:16 says, "All things were created by him, and for him." Consider the phrase "for him." We often think of God the Son coming to earth for us, and He did. But this verse says we came into being for Him. How should that shape our outlook?**

_____

_____

_____

_____

> **Paul states that "by him [Christ] all things consist" (Col. 1:17; see also Hebrews 1:3.) What does that mean, and how could it affect your daily outlook?**

_____

_____

_____

_____

The Sufficient Ministry of Christ

Have you ever looked up into the sky on a clear night and been overwhelmed by the incomprehensible immensity of space? How could the Creator of all that and more relate to me? How could I ever travel far enough to meet Him? If that were not enough of a dilemma, what about all of my guilt and shame and questions about why things on earth are not right?

The wonderful answer is that God did not wait for us to find a way to meet Him. He knew we never would, even though He has revealed Himself in all of creation. In eternity past God chose to come in person in "the fullness of time" (Gal. 4:4) so that we could know Him. And to know God and His Son "is life eternal" (John 17:3). Much of what Paul says about Christ in Colossians 1 focuses on His exalted status as Lord. But there is more. In Colossians 2 we see that Christ not only rules but also ministers. The incarnate God, Christ Jesus, is the mediator between God and men (1 Tim. 2:5). His ministry is all we need.

Christ Mediates the Knowledge of God

COLOSSIANS 2:2-4

> That their hearts might be comforted, being knit together in love, and unto all riches of the full assurance of understanding, to the acknowledgement of the mystery of God, and of the Father, and of Christ; in whom are hid all the treasures of wisdom and knowledge. And this I say, lest any man should beguile you with enticing words.

First, out of concern that the Colossians not be persuaded by plausible but false arguments, Paul underscores Christ's ministry as the source of divine knowledge. Knowledge gained through a personal relationship with Christ is sufficient (Col. 2:2–4). No additives are necessary, for Christ has brought to completion all the Old Testament shadows to which the false teaching appealed (2:17). To know Christ is to possess "wisdom and knowledge," which is to possess "treasures" (2:3). Again, Paul speaks to the dangerous fascination with mysteries. God did not deceptively withhold the truth from mankind but waited for "the fulness of time" to unveil Christ and His efficacy for Gentiles (Gal. 4:4). Such a wise, sovereign plan trumps any amateur attempt to gain spiritual favor through "the commandments and doctrine of men" (Col. 2:22).

Christ Mediates the Presence of God

COLOSSIANS 2:9
For in him dwelleth all the fulness of the Godhead bodily.

Second, Christ's sufficiency extends from His mediation of divine revelation to His incarnation of divine presence. Christ embodies "all the fulness" of deity (2:9). The incarnation was no dirty chore. God was well-pleased that the Son would dwell among men in the fullness of God (1:19). The wonder of the incarnation is that the Godhead fully knew the ramifications. The manger was not pleasant, but Christ came *to die*. John's words—that "the Word was made flesh, and dwelt among us" (John 1:14)—include tabernacle terminology. Just as the Shekhinah glory filled the tabernacle and temple, the full perfections of God the Father fill the Son, Jesus the Messiah. He lacks no part of God. Remember, Christ is God's very image. Even more remarkably, He who embodies the fullness of God fills us (Col. 2:10). The only way for sinners to be filled by the fullness of God is to be united to Christ through faith—to be incorporated into the body of which He is the Head. Christ is sufficient, perfect, and complete in His revelation of divine knowledge and in His embodiment of divine presence. We can have confidence that Christ is *more than enough.*

Christ Mediates the Salvation of God

COLOSSIANS 2:10–15
And ye are complete in him, which is the head of all principality and power: in whom also ye are circumcised with the circumcision made without hands, In putting off the body of the sins of the flesh by the circumcision of Christ: buried with him in baptism, wherein also ye are risen with him through the faith of the operation of God, who hath raised him from the dead. And you, being dead in your sins and the uncircumcision of your flesh, hath he quickened

> together with him, having forgiven you all tres-
> passes; blotting out the handwriting of ordinances
> that was against us, which was contrary to us, and
> took it out of the way, nailing it to his cross; and
> having spoiled principalities and powers, he made
> a shew of them openly, triumphing over them in it.

CHRIST'S ACTION ON BEHALF OF BELIEVERS IS SUFFICIENT TO FILL US UP. WE NEED NOT AND SHOULD NOT ADD TO CHRIST.

Third, Christ is more than adequate in His ministry as Savior. After Paul emphatically states, "ye are complete in Him" (2:10), he unfolds the glories of God's saving work in the following five verses, which serve as the theological high point of this letter. God saves us through Christ through spiritual circumcision, for Christ's death proved to be death for the flesh of those who trust Him (2:11). God also saves us by raising us to new life with Christ. His experience of God's resurrection power serves as the basis for our own spiritual life (2:12–13). Furthermore, God saves us by canceling our sin debt through the vicarious death of Christ, who is the end of the law's demands on us (2:14). Finally, God saves us by disarming and disrobing demonic powers and leading them in triumphal procession through the victory of Christ on the cross (2:15). In His greatest moment of weakness and vulnerability, Jesus Christ dealt the deathblow to man's mortal enemies: the legal decrees that condemn us and the demonic powers that wage war against our souls. Christ's action on behalf of believers is sufficient to fill us up. We need not and should not add to Christ. He is a perfect Savior.

▮▮ *Read Colossians 2:11–15. List the truths this passages teaches about salvation.*

_____

_____

_____

_____

_____

▮▮ *The sufficient ministry of Christ involves His mediating God's knowledge, presence, and salvation. Pick one of those three and discuss its importance for spiritual growth and maturity.*

_____

_____

_____

_____

Our Response to the Truth of Christ

COLOSSIANS 2:6–7

As ye have therefore received Christ Jesus the Lord, so walk ye in him: rooted and built up in him, and stablished in the faith, as ye have been taught, abounding therein with thanksgiving.

In light of the magnificent truth of Jesus Christ, it is no wonder that Paul exhorts his readers, "As ye have therefore received Christ Jesus the Lord, so walk ye in him" (2:6). Satan frequently tempts us to move past our Savior and look for direction and satisfaction in other things, even religious ones. The deceiver knows that our strength lies in our Savior (Eph. 6:10–18), not in what we add to Him.

The language Paul uses indicates we must *continue living* in Christ (Col. 2:6). What would that look like? Paul gives a four-fold answer in Colossians 2:7. First, we remain "rooted" in Christ. The Lord Himself said, "As the branch cannot bear fruit of itself, except it abide in the vine; no more can ye, except ye abide in me" (John 15:4). He is the only true source of nourishment and vitality. Second, we are being "built up in him." In other words, we are God's construction project, and Christ is not merely the architectural drawings. He is the structure and purpose of the building (see 1 Peter 2:5–8). Third, we are "stablished in the faith." Our Christian life does not begin with the gospel and then move on to other things. We "grow in grace, and in the knowledge of our Lord and Savior Jesus Christ" (2 Pet. 3:18). Walking in Christ means becoming increasingly established in the apostolic faith centered on Jesus Christ. Finally, walking in Christ means "abounding therein with thanksgiving" (Col. 2:7). When our hearts are gripped with the reality of Christ the supreme Lord and sufficient Savior, our tongues can do nothing less than thank Him.

The kind of true Christian living we will study in Colossians 3 is based on the fundamental truths of Jesus Christ in Colossians 1 and 2. He is the supreme Lord and the sufficient Savior. Our response is to submit to His preeminence over every area of our lives (Col. 1:18). This is a conscious decision and a personal commitment to give Christ first place. However, this is far more than an initial, one-time decision. It includes a heart and mind that is being daily transformed through a personal relationship with Christ. By God's grace we have received Him. By God's grace we must keep walking in Him.

What does it mean that Christ is "the firstborn of every creature" (Col. 1:15)? What about the designation "the firstborn from the dead" (Col. 1:18)?

Has your spiritual focus drifted away from Christ? Are you tempted to trust in other people or things for your satisfaction or approval?

In Colossians 2:6-7 Paul lists four ways that believers continue walking in Christ. Why do you think he listed thanksgiving last? What does that have to do with being grounded in the truth of Christ?

NOTES

03

THE BELIEVER'S IDENTITY

COLOSSIANS 3:1-4

If ye then be risen with Christ, seek those things which are above, where Christ sitteth on the right hand of God. Set your affection on things above, not on things on the earth. For ye are dead, and your life is hid with Christ in God. When Christ, who is our life, shall appear, then shall ye also appear with him in glory.

Credit card identify theft is one of the great crimes of the twenty-first century. Many have suffered from its cruel effects. Similarly, the first century believers living in the city of Colossae faced a crisis with spiritual identity theft. Certain erroneous teachers had come into the church and, through their message, were attempting to rob the believers of their identity in Christ.

Here was the scenario:

False teachers had come to the church with this basic message: The gospel they had received from Epaphras (1:7) was sufficient to save them, but it was insufficient to spiritually mature them. In other words, they could not reach their complete spiritual potential on the basis of the simple gospel message they had received. These teachers promised that their message would give the Colossian church the experience of a fuller spiritual life and greater freedom over their sinful natures. Their primary emphasis was a combination of seeking mystical experiences (perhaps with angels) to know God greater and of keeping religious rules and regulations, along with a strict, ascetic lifestyle to free themselves from the evil desires of their own sinful hearts.

BELIEVERS ARE ABSOLUTELY AND UNEQUIVOCALLY COMPLETE IN CHRIST ALONE.

The problem, however, is that their message was an aberration of the truth. These emphases do not result in greater knowledge and freedom but greater ignorance and bondage. In this letter to believers he had never met, Paul emphatically asserts that the gospel they had received was an all-sufficient message of Jesus Christ, an all-sufficient Savior. Believers are absolutely and unequivocally complete in Christ alone. So Paul's challenge was to not allow these spiritual identity thieves to rob the Colossians of who they were as men and women in Christ.

Colossians 3 is one of the finest statements in the whole of the Bible concerning the believer's identity being in Jesus Christ. In the first four verses Paul explains our identity in Christ from three perspectives: past, present, and future.

Our Past Identity in Christ

COLOSSIANS 2:12

Buried with him in baptism, wherein also ye are risen with him through the faith of the operation of God, who hath raised him from the dead.

First, Paul points back to the past when we died and were raised with Christ. In what way has the believer died with Christ? He becomes so much a part of Christ and His death that the believer actually dies, not physically but spiritually, with Christ. Paul explains this in the previous chapter by saying we were "buried with Him in baptism" (2:12). He also declares this in

Romans 6:3–4: "Know ye not, that so many of us as were baptized into Jesus Christ were baptized into his death? Therefore we are buried with him by baptism into death."

Our guilt is buried with Christ! Furthermore, believers have died to the elemental spiritual forces of this world.

> Wherefore if ye be dead with Christ from the rudiments of the world . . . (Col. 2:20)

The false teachers were trying to kidnap the believers. Their message gave an appearance of new wisdom. In reality their teaching was not new or wise. It was the same man-made, works-based religious message throughout the ages—of both Jews and Gentiles—that focuses on what a person has to perform in order to experience a spiritual life. Their message does not lead a believer into spiritual freedom but into spiritual bondage. In the end this teaching actually severs believers from the "Head," Jesus Christ. On the contrary, through Christ's death believers have died to these worldly religious principles.

But there is more. Our past identity in Christ involves not only death but life. We have risen to a living relationship with the Son of God.

> If ye then be risen with Christ . . . (Col. 3:1)

Every believer receives a new life and becomes a new creation.

> Ye are risen with him through the faith of the operation of God, who hath raised him from the dead. And you . . . hath he quickened together with him, having forgiven you all trespasses. (Col. 2:12–13)

We have been disconnected from the old world order and connected to a new heavenly order—the kingdom of God. We now share in the power of the risen life of their King! It is no wonder Paul urgently prayed for the Ephesians to understand the immensity of their privilege in possessing Christ's power.

> And what is the exceeding greatness of his power
> to us-ward who believe, according to the working of
> his mighty power, which he wrought in Christ, when
> he raised him from the dead, and set him at his own
> right hand in the heavenly places. (Eph. 1:19–20)

Christ is your new life source. This is who you are. This is your identity. Don't let anyone rob you of this!

What were some of the aspects of the false teaching? What makes the message of the false teachers so appealing?

_____

_____

_____

_____

_____

Our Present Identity in Christ

COLOSSIANS 3:1–3

> If ye then be risen with Christ, seek those things
> which are above, where Christ sitteth on the right
> hand of God. Set your affection on things above,
> not on things on the earth. For ye are dead, and
> your life is hid with Christ in God.

Secondly, God reveals that believers are identified with Christ in the present. The current identity of God's people is hidden with Christ. The verb for *hidden* (from which we get our English word *cryptic*) means encrypted or embedded. Believers' identity and status with God is virtually unseen by the world.

We are like Christ. Jesus was crucified in public view, but when He rose from the dead only His disciples saw Him. Afterward He ascended into heaven, sat down at the Father's right hand, and rules from a position of power and preeminence. He is the Head over all things, and everything has been placed under His feet. However, the world does not and cannot see this because they are blinded to Jesus.

Likewise, we are also hidden from the world's eyes. This is dramatically illustrated in Joseph, who was despised and rejected by his brothers and sold into slavery. In time, he was exalted to the king's right hand and given power over the nation. When his brothers came to him seeking to buy food, his identity was hidden from them until he revealed himself at the opportune time. This is the current state of all believers. The world doesn't understand what has happened in us through salvation, nor can they perceive what is going to happen to us.

> Beloved, now are we the sons of God, and it doth not yet appear what we shall be: but we know that, when he shall appear, we shall be like him; for we shall see him as he is (1 John 3:2).

Therefore, we are presently waiting with a confident anticipation that the day will come when heaven will open, Christ will return, and we will be seen for who we are in Christ. This is our hope!

Our lives are secure with Christ (Col. 3:3). People may think we are just ordinary people with a delusive dream, but our eternal life is actually as secure as the existence of God Himself.

Describe the struggles a Christian may have with accepting his/her identity in Christ rather than finding identity in the world and its attractions. How does the word hid *in Colossians 3:3 help?*

_____

_____

_____

_____

_____

Our Future Identity in Christ

COLOSSIANS 3:4

When Christ, who is our life, shall appear, then shall
ye also appear with him in glory.

Finally, Paul explains that believers are identified with Christ
in the future. When Jesus returns, the whole world will be cap-
tivated by His glory. They will recognize that He is Lord. They
will bow before Him and confess Him for who He is. They will
also see believers for who we are and will suddenly perceive
the power that energized our lives and the values that moti-
vated us. In the present, we suffer with Him. In the future, we
will share in His glory.

> For I reckon that the sufferings of this present time
> are not worthy to be compared with the glory
> which shall be revealed in us. (Romans 8:18)

Our association with Christ for eternity could not be closer.
We will "appear with him" (Col. 3:4).

Discuss the importance of establishing your identity in Christ. What difference does it make?

_____

_____

_____

_____

_____

Conclusion

As we studied in the last chapter, the essence of Christianity is Christ Himself. He "is our life" (Col. 3:4).

- Consider His person—"he is the head of the body, the church," (1:18)

- Consider His performance—He triumphed over sin and all evil powers (2:11–15)

- Consider God's promises about Him—"ye also appear with him in glory" (3:4)

- Consider our position in Him—"your life is hid with Christ in God" (3:3)

LIVING THE CHRISTIAN LIFE HAS EVERYTHING TO DO WITH SCRIPTURE'S DECLARATIONS ABOUT CHRIST AND OUR IDENTITY WITH HIM.

Living the Christian life has everything to do with Scripture's declarations about Christ and our identity with Him.

Jesus is the answer, whether the issue is

spiritual wisdom, church leadership, reconciliation, our standing before a holy God, focus in ministry, the weight of transgressions, demonic power, victory over sexual temptation, sinful communication patterns, disunity and selfishness, or open doors for ministry. Jesus is the answer, and we are fully identified with Him. We cannot look for satisfaction in stuff or groups or experiences or achievements. They easily rob us of who we truly are. Our identity is Jesus Christ.

Paul states that Christ "is our life" (Col. 3:4). Look back at Colossians 1–2 and list the truths about Christ that make our full identification with Him so amazing.

_____

_____

_____

_____

How is the believer raised with Christ? How could meditating on the truth of your resurrected life in Christ make a substantial difference in your everyday experience?

_____

_____

_____

_____

How often do you think about the second coming of Christ? Why is it important that you do?

NOTES

04

THE BELIEVER'S FOCUS

COLOSSIANS 3:1–2
If ye then be risen with Christ, seek those things which are
above, where Christ sitteth on the right hand of God. Set your
affection on things above, not on things on the earth.

Jonathan Edwards is considered the greatest theological mind in American history. He was also one of the key leaders of the Great Awakening of the 1730s. During this period of revival there were many conversions. These new believers organized themselves into small groups for prayer, singing, accountability, and encouragement. People became intense, zealous, and earnest about their faith. Unfortunately, there were some emotional excesses that took place. As a result, a group of pastors arose who opposed the revival. They began to speak out against it, creating a division among colonial evangelicals. Those who supported the revival were called the New Lights, and those who opposed it were called the Old Lights.

The distinction between these two groups was subtle, but there were immense differences in the way the two groups approached Christian living and worship. The primary difference had to do with the mind. Both groups agreed that Scripture was their authority and that God renews and utilizes human reasoning. However, there was a distinction in the way the two groups viewed the affections. Edwards emphasized that the intellect without true affections is an insufficient spirituality. In other words, when the Holy Spirit awakens someone, God renews not only his intellect but also his affections (or righteous desires). The Old Lights were suspicious of an outwardly emotional faith. They proposed that the guide for all religious affairs should be an enlightened mind and not elevated affections. They associated the affections with the passions of one's lower nature that needed to be restrained by the higher faculty of reason.

Navigating this debate is still important today. We distinguish spiritual passion from mere intellectualism. Or, to put it simply, we believe that we should have a heart and passion for God. But this does not negate the mind. Rather, when the mind is fully engaged with the things of God, a proper passion will arise in the heart.

Out of this conflict, Edwards wrote what is considered a masterpiece in the history of Christian literature, *A Treatise on Religious Affections*. His main point was, "True religion consists, in a great measure, in vigorous and lively actings of the inclination and will of the soul, or the fervent exercises of the heart."[1]

The essence of what Edwards writes is the same basic truth that Paul was expressing in Colossians 3:1–4: True spirituality is a passionate pursuit of heavenly realities. Because our true identity is in Christ, who is above, we must focus our will and affections on things above—in other words, on what is heavenly and eternal.

---

[1] Jonathan Edwards, *The Works of President Edwards* (New York: Leavitt, Trow & Co., 1844), 3:5.

Seek Things Above

Paul directs our focus with two commands. First, he exhorts us to pursue heavenly realities with all our hearts. The term *seek* means to search purposefully. It signifies an urgent quest that engages our will. We are to be as earnest in seeking Christ as the shepherd who sought his lost sheep or the woman who sought her lost coin or the father who sought his lost son (Luke 15).

The center of our intense search must be Christ Himself. The heresy in Colossae promised spiritual fulfillment through keeping Old Testament laws and regulations. However, these were only pictures pointing to Christ, the fulfillment and end of the law (Rom. 10:4). Imagine a soldier taking pictures of his wife and children to war. Upon his safe return home, whom does the soldier want to hug and kiss? Would it be his wife and kids or pictures of them? Fill your hearts with Christ. The more you pursue Him, the more you will want to pursue Him. Christ is to be the center and source of all our joys. We must be personally convinced, as Paul was, that "to live is Christ, and to die is gain" (Phil. 1:21).

> COMMITMENT TO PURSUING CHRIST MEANS LIVING IN THE REALITY OF HIS PREEMINENCE OVER ALL THINGS.

As we delight in Christ and our position in Him, it is critical that we recognize what position Christ Himself is in. He sits "on the right hand of God" (Col. 3:1). He is Lord! Commitment to pursuing Christ means living in the reality of His preeminence over all things. We are to dedicate every area of our lives to His loving Lordship so that we entrust to Him our entire future, family, finances, and friendships along

SEEKING THINGS ABOVE: A STUDY IN COLOSSIANS

with our talents, time, and treasures—all of these to Him. We cannot revel in the *benefits package* of our position in Christ and forget the related obligations of being a servant of Christ.

Set Your Affections on Things Above

COLOSSIANS 3:2

Set your affection on things above, not on things on the earth.

Secondly, Paul exhorts us to develop a mindset of singular devotion that believes and embraces the rule of Christ over our lives. In order to demonstrate heavenly conduct, we must adopt a heavenly outlook. True spirituality requires choices about what we think and love. It is very difficult to seek things above when our affections are somewhere else.

PAUL CHARGES US NOT TO SET OUR AFFECTIONS ON THE THINGS THAT ROB US OF A HEART FOR CHRIST.

In this letter Paul charges us not to set our affections on the things that rob us of a heart for Christ. He warns us of the spiritual dead-end street of mystical pursuits and legalistic rules. He also commands us to ruthlessly deny ourselves mind-controlling sexual thoughts. These are to be totally abandoned for Christ. Paul urges us to fix our thoughts on our identity in Christ. We are to believe what God says about us and constantly adjust our thinking to that reality.

It is noteworthy that Paul aims to capture the gaze of our affections. Thomas Chalmers, a well-known Scottish theologian of the nineteenth century, wrote a message entitled *The Expulsive*

Power of a New Affection. Chalmers's premise is that it is virtually impossible to displace love for something evil simply by exposing it as empty and worthless. An effective change can come only when you set forth another object, in this case, God, who is more worthy of one's heart affection and attachment. He states, "The heart shall be prevailed upon not to resign an old affection, which shall have nothing to succeed it, but to exchange an old affection for a new one."[2]

In other words, we could spend a lot of time telling ourselves to stop thinking about ourselves so much. We could vow to deprive ourselves of legitimate joys and beat ourselves up, literally or figuratively. Or we could start spending a lot more time making God's Word at home in our lives and thereby treasuring Jesus Christ. We have so much trouble fighting sin, not usually because we do not know what is wrong with it, but because we do not have a more powerful loyalty and affection for Christ to overwhelm it.

Discuss what a passion for Christ looks like. Are there any verses that describe this passion? What would cultivate such passion in your life this coming week?

---

[2]Thomas Chalmers, "The Expulsive Power of a New Affection," in *Master Sermons of the Nineteenth Century*, ed. Gaius Glenn Atkins (New York: Clark, 1940), 4.

> **Discuss "the expulsive power of a new affection." Share examples of how powerful this truth could be.**

_____

_____

_____

_____

_____

Conclusion

Errant theology often promises heavenly blessings detached from earthly obligations. For example, the ancient Gnostics viewed the body as inherently evil material, whereas the realm of the mind is inherently good and spiritual. Consequently, some Gnostics entertained spectacular meditations on mystical ideas but were quite sinful in their lifestyle. Like the false teacher in Colossae, they had devised methods of creating a virtual heaven removed from moral responsibilities.

As we will repeatedly discover in the following chapters of this study, life in Christ is focused above but takes place here below. Christianity is not escaping to virtual reality but bringing heavenly reality to earth. Paul says we must seek and set our affections on what is above, but that does not mean we ignore earthly realities. We should watch the balance of our checking accounts and give some thought to our appearance and study biology and socialize with friends. But there are two common pitfalls. On one hand it is easy to view earthly pursuits as the primary reality and not passionately seek Christ day by day. On the other hand it is tempting to assume we are Christ-centered because we have good theory when our actual speech and behavior indicate otherwise. Seeking things above is true Christianity—a practical life of pleasing the Lord (see

Eph. 5:10). If Christ is our life, we must pursue Him earnestly, adopt His mindset, and apply His grace to everyday living here and now.

What does Paul mean by his command to seek (Col. 3:1)? What about the command to "set your affection on things above" (Col. 3:2)? How are they related?

_____

_____

_____

_____

Does your relationship with Christ tend to be intellectual (knowledge of the truth), emotional (passionate experience), or ethical (making right choices)? Colossians 3 shows how all three are important. Write down one truth from this study that would help cultivate the aspects of this relationship that may be lacking.

_____

_____

_____

_____

Jesus is Lord, seated "on the right hand of God" (Col. 3:1). Do you tend to view Him this way? If not, what about your life might change if you did?

_____

_____

_____

_____

_____

Do you tend to focus on earthly realities and forget about the eternal? Which ones? What have you learned about Christ in this study that would help you focus on heavenly realities?

_____

_____

_____

_____

_____

NOTES

05

UNDERSTANDING SIN

COLOSSIANS 3:5-10

Mortify therefore your members which are upon the earth; fornication, uncleanness, inordinate affection, evil concupiscence, and covetousness, which is idolatry: for which things' sake the wrath of God cometh on the children of disobedience: in the which ye also walked some time, when ye lived in them. But now ye also put off all these; anger, wrath, malice, blasphemy, filthy communication out of your mouth. Lie not one to another, seeing that ye have put off the old man with his deeds; and have put on the new man, which is renewed in knowledge after the image of him that created him:

In his book *God's Words*, J. I. Packer writes, "Our first need in life is to learn about sin. . . . If you have not learned about sin, you cannot understand yourself, or your fellow men, or the world you live in, or the Christian faith. And you will not be able to make head or tail of the Bible."[1] He is right. Understanding sin is crucial in starting the Christian life and in continuing the Christian life.

Perhaps we do not have a clear view of sin because it is such a hideous picture. It is like a doctor showing his patient a photo of clogged arteries. We would prefer simply not to see what our diet choices are doing to our bodies. However, ignoring the facts does not make them go away. Similarly, the power of positive thinking is no match for a reality that God describes

---

[1] J. I. Packer, *God's Words* (Downers Grove, IL: InterVarsity Press, 1981), 71.

with words like *disobedience, lawlessness, iniquity, wickedness, trespass, transgression,* and *rebellion.* Some people suggest that the categories of *good* and *evil* do not even exist. But when we look around us, the terrible reality is undeniable.

The truth about sin is not only repulsive, it is also personal. It is easy to read the account of Adam and Eve in the garden and wonder how perfect people could be misled. But how many lies of the devil have we believed in the last week? The news regularly reports brutal, premeditated murders. But then again, professing believers whose anger is kindled toward brothers are "in danger of the judgment" (Matt. 5:22). We read the account of David and Bathsheba and shake our heads in disapproval. But Jesus said that to look with lust is to commit adultery in the heart (Matt. 5:28). Sin is not other people's problem. It is ours. "There is none righteous, no, not one" (Rom. 3:10).

SEEKING THINGS ABOVE HAS DEFINITE IMPLICATIONS FOR DEALING WITH SIN BELOW.

Consequently, seeking things above has definite implications for dealing with sin below. That is why Paul moves from the importance of our affections to the necessity of understanding and overcoming our sin. This chapter examines Paul's teaching about sin, while the following chapter focuses on overcoming it.

Sexual Sins

COLOSSIANS 3:5

Mortify therefore your members which are upon the earth; fornication, uncleanness, inordinate affection, evil concupiscence, and covetousness,

Unsurprisingly, Paul first takes aim at immorality and greed. The Colossians did not face unique, uncommon battles. This instruction is for all of us. For one thing, Paul instructed them to pass this letter along to Laodicea. In addition, this letter has been circulating for nearly two thousand years now. Instead, the apostle exposes the evil of sexual temptations because they lie near the heart of our adversary's attack. If we want to experience growth in Christ, we have to draw some sober conclusions about moral purity.

Most of us are very aware of the onslaught of sensuality that barrages our eyes and minds every day. The devastating effects of our super-sexed society are evident across a range of issues, including pornography, divorce, abortion, births out of wedlock, sexual assault, and child abuse, to name only a few. But even though our contemporary context is very challenging, the problem isn't fundamentally our godless culture or twenty-first-century technology. Jesus Himself said that what comes out of a person's own heart is what defiles him (Mark 7:20–22).

Many reject conclusions like Paul's and Jesus Christ's, raising questions such as, "What is the big deal? If I'm not hurting anyone, why does it matter?" It matters because immoral sins are thoughts and actions that pervert one of God's best gifts—sexuality. Sex was designed to be part of the marriage experience and to enhance the love of a husband and wife. Satan has taken this good gift and distorted it through self-centered corruption. He has turned love into lust. Paul catalogs these sexual sins in Colossians 3:5 and expects all believers to radically turn away from them.

Paul calls them "your members which are upon the earth" (3:5). He is not saying that our physical bodies are inherently evil. That demonic lie contradicts Scripture's clear teaching (1 Tim. 4:3–4). After all, God created all of us, and pronounced the entirety of His creation "very good" (Gen. 1:31). Instead, the problem is that people typically use their bodies to serve sin (Rom. 6:19). We think, "It's my body, and I'll do as I want to." It is an earthly, man-centered mindset, rather than an eternal, God-centered one.

Paul candidly names five vices:

- **fornication:** any sexual activity outside of marriage

- **uncleanness:** impurity; moral corruption (e.g., pornography)

- **inordinate affection:** habitual lust; shameful passion

- **evil concupiscence:** misdirected fulfillment of natural desires

- **covetousness:** greed that is the source for sexual sin

Whether arousing sexual contact outside of marriage, or looking at provocative images, or masturbating, or reading sensual novels, or engaging in locker-room humor, or sexting—it's all in this list.

Where does *idolatry* fit in? A dissatisfied and greedy heart is fertile soil for the kinds of moral impurity that Paul lists first. Furthermore, false religion and immorality go together, not just in the ancient world of Canaan or Colossae. Think of the sexual liberty promoted by liberal churches. Think of the moral freedom demanded by contemporary atheism. Think of what is cherished on most college campuses—football, alcohol, and free sex. The mantra is: *You're free to hook up.* This is the way the world "walks." This is who people are outside of Christ (Col. 3:7). By contrast, heaven-focused, Christ-centered living pursues moral purity.

Why does Paul transition from the eternal mindset of Colossians 3:1–4 to focus on sexual sins in verses 5–7?

_____

_____

_____

_____

_____

Read Matthew 5:27–28 and Ephesians 5:3–5. Discuss the difference between God's perspective on sexual sin and the world's.

_____

_____

_____

_____

Speech Sins

COLOSSIANS 3:8

But now ye also put off all these; anger, wrath, malice, blasphemy, filthy communication out of your mouth.

Paul proceeds to a second category, commanding us to confess the sins committed by our tongues. In Colossians 3:8–9 he focuses on verbal reactions that disrupt and damage interpersonal relationships within one's family, church, and society.

We use words so frequently and freely that we tend to underestimate their significance. It is convenient for us to section off

THE REALITY IS THAT WHAT WE SAY AND WHAT WE TYPE HAS EVERYTHING TO DO WITH WHO WE ARE AND WHAT WE REALLY VALUE IN LIFE. our words as something separate from what we really are. Or we think of our tongues as committing "respectable sins."[2] But the reality is that what we say and what we type has everything to do with who we are and what we really value in life. Sins of the mouth always reveal the state of one's heart: "for out of the abundance of the heart the mouth speaketh" (Matt. 12:34).

Paul again lists a series of sins. The first three commonly lead to the last two. As you read these descriptions, think of the ways such sins contradict the message that Christ is our life.

- **anger:** smoldering, chronic irritation that leads to resentment, bitterness, or sarcasm

- **wrath:** flaring, passionate outburst (Col. 3:8)

- **malice:** badness; hostility and hatefulness that lead to vicious speech

- **blasphemy:** slander, such as lies, gossip, or defamation of character

- **filthy communication out of your mouth:** vulgar or obscene speech that abuses

Paul seems to single out one very obvious manifestation of corrupt communication among a community of believers: "Lie not one to another" (Col. 3:9). Notice the corporate aspect of

---

[2]See the probing book by Jerry Bridges, *Respectable Sins: Confronting the Sins We Tolerate* (Colorado Spring: NavPress, 2007).

this command. We have a responsibility to *one another*. Lying disrupts the intended unity of Christ's body. It is destructive. "Fellowship is built on trust, and trust is built on truth."[3] In other words, unity is a wonderful thing, but it cannot merely be tolerance of everyone and everything. It is centered on what is true because Christianity hinges on truth. Christ told Pilate that He came into the world to testify to the truth (John 18:36–37). He is "the Word" (1:1) and it is by His truth that we are set free (8:32). Therefore, by speaking the truth we build up one another (Eph. 4:29).

This imperative covers more accepted forms of deceit such as evasion and insinuation and exaggeration. Integrity and humility matter in communication, not as isolated virtues of a bygone era, but as weighty testimony to the trustworthy character of our Lord. Perhaps speech sins are not as notorious as sexual sins, but they can be just as destructive. Jesus' half-brother James wrote, "And the tongue *is* a fire, a world of iniquity: so is the tongue among our members, that it defileth the whole body, and setteth on fire the course of nature; and it is set on fire of hell" (James 3:6). Living with an eternal, Christ-centered focus means viewing what we say exactly as God does.

> *Look at the definition of* **anger** *above. What are common evidences of anger among Christians?*

_____

_____

_____

---

[3]John R. W. Stott, *The Message of Ephesians*, The Bible Speaks Today, ed. John R. W. Stott (Downers Grove, Ill.: Inter-Varsity Press, 1979), 185.

When the term blasphemy *is directed at other people, it means* slander. *This word also appears in Ephesians 4:31 as* evil speaking. *Discuss the definition listed above and what Paul (in Ephesians 4:31–5:2) counsels us to do about it.*

Divine Wrath

COLOSSIANS 3:6

For which things' sake the wrath of God cometh on the children of disobedience.

In order to understand what Paul teaches about sin, we must consider one more aspect of these verses. It is important to realize that Paul is not merely pointing out the social damage done by sexual and speech sins. Many unbelievers would agree that sexual misconduct and anger and lying can have disastrous effects. But as sobering as the horizontal implications are, Paul's point is deeper. Fundamentally, there is a God (Eph. 4:6). He created us, and He is holy. And because He is holy, He must demonstrate wrath. This is not erratic, vindictive anger. It is God's settled antagonism toward all that violates the righteousness and beauty and peace that He is and that He intends for us. God would not be good if He did not deal with evil.

Romans 1 tells us that His wrath is already revealed from heaven against our unrighteousness, which starts by sinners suppressing truth about Him. When we as sinners give way to idolatry, we set ourselves up for greed, and He gives us over to fulfill our lustful passions. He has *already* revealed wrath against this kind of living (Rom. 1:18). It "cometh on the children of disobedience" (Col. 3:6). And the final judgment of condemnation is imminent—it's on the way—for those who refuse to repent. If we want to seek things above, we have to take a sobering look at sin in high definition.

> *Do you reflect much on the nature of sin? Take one of the words mentioned in the introduction of this chapter and think about it in relation to your sin this past week—disobedience, lawlessness, iniquity, wickedness, trespass, transgression, and rebellion.*

_____

_____

_____

_____

> *Are you facing sexual temptation? Is the temptation coming through a certain relationship or electronic device or pattern in life? Are you taking God's side against this temptation? Or are you caving in to the world's mindset? Do you need to go to someone for help?*

_____

_____

_____

_____

_____

Which of the speech sins listed by Paul is/are a struggle for you? Has there been a recent incident that you need to make right with God and other people?

_____

_____

_____

_____

_____

NOTES

06

OVERCOMING SIN

COLOSSIANS 3:5–10
Mortify therefore your members which are upon the
earth; fornication, uncleanness, inordinate affection, evil
concupiscence, and covetousness, which is idolatry: for which
things' sake the wrath of God cometh on the children of
disobedience: in the which ye also walked some time, when ye
lived in them. But now ye also put off all these; anger, wrath,
malice, blasphemy, filthy communication out of your mouth. Lie
not one to another, seeing that ye have put off the old man with
his deeds; and have put on the new man, which is renewed in
knowledge after the image of him that created him.

Occasionally public outrage erupts about a big-game
hunter who kills an endangered species.[1] Obeying regulations, hunting or otherwise, is certainly important. But for
many in the history of the world, predatory animals have had
little to do with licenses and expensive sport. Instead, they
have presented a very dangerous dilemma. An encounter with
a lion, for instance, left a person with only two choices: kill it,
or it will kill you.

Did you realize that this is exactly the challenge we face in our
spiritual lives? John Owen, seventeenth century Puritan and
Oxford vice-chancellor, is credited with this famous statement:

---

[1]For example, see http://www.nytimes.com/2015/07/29/world/africa/
american-hunter-is-accused-of-killing-cecil-a-beloved-lion-in-zimbabwe.
html?_r=0.

SIN IS A PREDATOR. IT CANNOT BE CODDLED. IT MUST BE ATTACKED.

"Be killing sin, or it will be killing you."[2] That jars our modern sensibilities. We usually want to think of our Christianity in much cheerier ways. But Owen knew sin is no small matter. Neutrality and passivity will not work. Sin is a predator. It cannot be coddled. It must be attacked.

One of the questions Paul answers in his letter to the Colossians is, "How can a believer overcome sin in his life?" He needed to address this issue because the aberrant message of the false teachers focused on keeping rules, denying legitimate bodily appetites, and gaining an inside track through angelic mediators. Their approach was external and legal. Paul, however, strongly emphasized the internal and spiritual, rooted in Christ's work on the cross.

This question is crucial for at least two reasons. First of all, overcoming sin is crucial to the spiritual maturity of the church. Growing in the knowledge of Jesus Christ requires the commitment to put away the sins of one's thoughts, attitudes, actions, and relationships. Sinful habits that linger stunt our personal growth. Most of Paul's letters were written to address some form of sin that was disrupting the unity, harmony, and maturity of the church. God's power and presence in the church is conditional based on the church's purity (1 Cor. 5:7–8; 1 John 1:5–7). A failure to overcome sin will eventually devastate the spiritual life of the church.

---

[2]John Owen, *The Works of John Owen*, ed. William H. Goold, 24 vols. (Edinburgh: Johnstone & Hunter, 1850–1855; reprint by Banner of Truth Trust, 1965, 1991), 6:9.

Second, overcoming sin is always relevant to our own Christian lives. All believers intensely struggle with the presence of indwelling sin (Rom. 7:14–25). Even the most mature believers keep coming back to the basics of how to overcome sin in their lives (Phil. 3:15). Preaching on sin is never out of date!

Overcoming sin is a lesson for all believers. Paul explains that the Colossian church was being taught to overcome sin in a wrong way. Therefore, in Colossians 3:5–9, he presents three foundational steps for overcoming sin. We studied the first step in the last chapter. Overcoming sin begins with understanding and admitting what sin truly is. In this chapter we will consider the other two steps—accept what is true, and act on what is true. Or to use Pauline language—believe and mortify.

Accept What Is True

COLOSSIANS 3:9–10

Lie not one to another, seeing that ye have put off the old man with his deeds; and have put on the new man, which is renewed in knowledge after the image of him that created him.

WORD STUDY

wrath—anger exhibited in punishment; righteous indignation (3:6)

walked—conducted one's self; made use of one's opportunities

put off—to put away; cast off; lay apart

put on—to clothe one's self; to sink into clothing

renewed—invigorated; strengthened

knowledge—comprehensive knowledge; full discernment or acknowledgement

image—moral likeness of Jesus Christ, the Son

Overcoming sin begins with accepting what God the Father has done in our lives through Jesus Christ. God has wrought a dramatic change in the life of every believer! The old man (our pre-conversion state) has been completely "put off" (3:9) at the moment of salvation. A miraculous transformation has taken place, and we are new men and women in Christ. Paul provides motivation to trust God and, therefore, overcome sin by explaining three powerful truths.

Deliverance from Divine Wrath

COLOSSIANS 1:13–14

Who hath delivered us from the power of darkness, and hath translated us into the kingdom of his dear Son: in whom we have redemption through his blood, even the forgiveness of sins.

First of all, we must accept that we have been delivered from God's wrath. Prior to their conversion, these Colossian believers practiced the kinds of immoral sins that provoke God's righteous wrath (3:7). However, through a sinner's faith in Christ God changes everything! Believers have been delivered from the domain of darkness (1:13). Jesus Christ has suffered God's wrath against sin by His death on the cross (1:21–22). Paul is now commanding believers to stop the very actions that were the cause of God's wrath by having confidence that Jesus Christ suffered that wrath in our place.

Severance from Our Old Self

COLOSSIANS 2:11–12

In whom also ye are circumcised with the circumcision made without hands, in putting off the body of the sins of the flesh by the circumcision of Christ: buried with him in baptism, wherein also ye are

risen with him through the faith of the operation of
God, who hath raised him from the dead.

We must also believe that we have been severed from the
power of the old life of sin. In this letter Paul describes this
experience of freedom in three symbols: circumcision, baptism, and changing clothes. First, he declares that believers
are spiritually circumcised (2:11). Circumcision was the cer-
emonial sign of the Abrahamic Covenant. It later symbolized
a Jew's dedication to God and separation from sin. In the New
Testament, circumcision is spiritual in nature and speaks of
the cutting off of the enslaving power of the old life and the do-
minion of sin. We are now able to overcome the lustful desires
of our sin nature (flesh) because of the circumcision of Christ.
Second, Paul announces that believers were buried with Christ
in baptism (2:12). Baptism symbolizes the death, burial, and
resurrection of Christ. To be baptized is to be initiated or im-
mersed into Christ. Therefore, through baptism we are united
or connected to Christ, and our old sinful life is buried with
Him. It's dead and gone! Third, Paul states that the old life is
put off like the changing of one's clothes (3:9). The old, worn
out, tattered sinful life has been set aside and exchanged for a
whole new life in Christ symbolized in new clothes.

All three images illustrate God's severing us from our old life
of sin. Have you ever watched someone apply a chain saw to
the trunk of a tree? Once he is finished, there is no vital connection between the tree and the stump. The tree removal pro-
fessional could plop the trunk back on its former base, but
their former relationship has been forever destroyed, never to
be restored. Praise God, that is what all who are in Christ have
experienced through His death and resurrection!

Identity As a New Creation in Christ

COLOSSIANS 3:10–11

And have put on the new man, which is renewed in knowledge after the image of him that created him: where there is neither Greek nor Jew, circumcision nor uncircumcision, Barbarian, Scythian, bond nor free: but Christ is all, and in all.

Finally, Paul provides motivation to overcome sin on the basis of our relationship to the church. We must believe that both we individually and the church corporately are God's new creations. We must forsake sin because it disrupts the harmony and maturity of the church. Overcoming sin is not just for the sake of one's own personal sanctification, but for the sake of the church, whom Christ purchased with His blood.

REGARDLESS OF RACE OR SOCIOECONOMIC STATUS OR FORMER RELIGION, CHRIST INDWELLS AND TRANSFORMS ALL WHO BELIEVE.

All believers have been recreated into a new image (3:10). Man's original creation in the likeness of God was lost by Adam through sin but was regained through Christ. As we studied in an earlier chapter, Paul describes Christ as the creator of the physical world and the spiritual church (1:15–20). The church is called the new creation made in the likeness or image of Jesus Christ. Furthermore, this new life has no cultural or class distinctions (3:11). Regardless of race or socioeconomic status or former religion, Christ indwells and transforms all who believe!

Everyone who is in Christ has been delivered from God's wrath, severed from the old life, and renovated into the new image of Christ. Therefore, we must accept who we are in Christ and live out that identity to overcome indwelling sin.

> **Read Ephesians 2:1–3 and 4:17–19. What do we need to accept about ourselves as sinners and about the unsaved world for the gospel of Jesus to be truly good news?**

_____

_____

_____

_____

> **How is God's work on your behalf totally sufficient for overcoming sin? Which of the three powerful truths listed above have you not been accepting in everyday life?**

_____

_____

_____

_____

Act on What Is True

The foundation of the Christian life is accepting the truth about who Christ is and what He has accomplished. But is that our only obligation? Actually, Paul states two commands in this section that compel us to action flowing from our faith. In other words, this is an *active* faith. Paul exhorts us to put sin to death (Col. 3:5) and to put sin away (3:8).

Kill It

COLOSSIANS 3:5

Mortify therefore your members which are upon the earth; fornication, uncleanness, inordinate affection, evil concupiscence, and covetousness, which is idolatry.

Mortification is actually where Paul's instruction concerning overcoming sin begins. The first word of Colossians 3:5 is *mortify*, which means "put to death." Paul also uses this image (though a different Greek verb) in Romans 8:13, saying, "but if ye through the Spirit do mortify the deeds of the body, ye shall live." (In fact, this is the passage that served as the basis of John Owen's classic *Of the Mortification of Sin in Believers*.)

The implication is obvious. It is great if the fans in the stands are chanting, "I believe that we will win!" But if their team does not control the ball and play defense, that belief becomes empty. We must wage an all-out war against our flesh. Passivity and tolerance on our part will result in spiritual defeat every time, because God requires that we not only accept what is true but act on it too.

Impurity characterizes the old way of life (3:7) and should have no part of our new position in Christ. Immorality and pornography and lust and greed are completely antithetical to the gospel. Therefore, every thought or act of immorality that was permitted in one's old life must receive a death sentence and be executed. Jesus uses the same language when He commands radical surgery with regards to sin: "If thy hand offend thee, cut it off: . . . and if thine eye offend thee, pluck it out" (Mark 9:43, 47).

Remove It

COLOSSIANS 3:8

But now ye also put off all these; anger, wrath, malice, blasphemy, filthy communication out of your mouth.

In addition to the image of putting sin to death, Paul commands us to put sin away. He compares this act of faith to one who changes a set of old, worn-out clothes for a new wardrobe. The attire of the old life includes anger, wrath, malice, slander, obscene talk, and lying. The power to change is found in the new life in the Spirit. Praise, prayer, and thanksgiving become the new responses to the situations and circumstances of life.

Again, Paul's exhortation is rooted in existing realities. We the people of God have "put off the old man" (3:9) and "put on the new man" (3:10). In other words, this wardrobe transformation has already occurred. A righteous Savior took the place of unrighteous sinners. As the modern hymn states, "His robes for mine, O wonderful exchange."[3] Unlike in Mark Twain's novel *The Prince and the Pauper* where two boys swap clothes and understandably spark confusion, salvation results in more than an external apparel trade. Our identity truly is transformed. It is as if Tom actually became and lived forever as Edward VI, king of England.

So why does Paul say in Colossians 3:8, "But now ye also put off all these"? If we have stripped off the old man already, why would we need to remove sin anymore? The answer is that even after the old man dies, sin continues to dog us. It is a defeated foe, but not an obliterated one. In fact, Paul himself confessed, "For the good that I would I do not: but the evil which I would not, that I do" (Rom. 7:19). Until we are glorified with Christ,

---

[3]Chris Anderson, "His Robes for Mine" Church Works Media, http://churchworksmedia.com/his-robes-for-mine, 2008. Used with permission.

SEEKING THINGS ABOVE: A STUDY IN COLOSSIANS

our flesh continues to fight against God's indwelling Spirit to draw us back into the sins that characterize the unsaved world (see Gal. 5:16–25). We must walk in the Spirit and continually shed the sins of our flesh.

The verb **put off** *occurs in several important New Testament contexts dealing with our changed lives as Christians. Look up the following references and summarize what they teach.*

Romans 13:12

_____

_____

Ephesians 4:22, 25

_____

_____

Hebrews 12:1

_____

_____

James 1:21

_____

_____

1 Peter 2:1

_____

_____

Discuss what it would look like this coming week to mortify and put off besetting sins this week. Think through the applications for yourself and for helping one another.

_____

_____

_____

_____

Ever since Adam and Eve listened to the serpent and pitted themselves against God, humanity has wrestled with sin. It seems like an untamed beast. But the good news is that in Christ we can overcome sin, dealing it blow after blow by acknowledging its true nature, accepting God's saving work, and actively living out our faith.

Can you give biblical counsel to someone who wants to overcome sin? What would you say?

_____

_____

_____

_____

Isaiah 61:10 speaks of salvation using the beautiful imagery of exquisite garments and robes. This alludes to the doctrine of substitutionary atonement. As a means of rehearsing the gospel, write out in your own words the doctrine of justification.

_____

NOTES

07

THE NATURE OF THE CHURCH

COLOSSIANS 3:10–13

And have put on the new man, which is renewed in knowledge after the image of him that created him: where there is neither Greek nor Jew, circumcision nor uncircumcision, Barbarian, Scythian, bond nor free: but Christ is all, and in all. Put on therefore, as the elect of God, holy and beloved, bowels of mercies, kindness, humbleness of mind, meekness, longsuffering; forbearing one another, and forgiving one another, if any man have a quarrel against any: even as Christ forgave you, so also do ye.

Scientific research shows that having a connection to something bigger than ourselves makes us happier and healthier.[1] New York Times columnist David Brooks gave advice to college graduates in a column he wrote entitled, "It's Not About You." His conclusion is that "The purpose in life is not to find yourself. It is to lose yourself."[2] He implies that the most successful people spend time on things bigger than themselves.

A part of Paul's ministry was to unveil to Gentile believers the fact that they are a part of something bigger than themselves— the church. Paul called the church a mystery. This refers to something hidden in the past but now revealed in the present. Old Testament Jews would not have understood the church. It was Paul whom God gave a stewardship to teach and explain the church. The secret he revealed was that believing Gentiles

---

[1]Seligman, M. E. P. *Flourish: A Visionary New Understanding of Happiness and Well-being* (New York: Free Press, 2011), 208.
[2]David Brooks, "It's Not About You," *New York Times*, May 30, 2011.

enter into the blessings of God's covenant reserved for the Jews through the gospel. Through the gospel they have become fellow heirs and partakers of all of God's promises (Eph. 3:1–6). Through the gospel they have been incorporated into the body of Christ, which is called the church (Col. 1:24). Through the gospel all believers are connected to their Head, Jesus Christ. Through the gospel, they are a part of something far bigger than themselves. So what is the nature of the church? Paul describes it with two powerful metaphors and a common way of life.

The New Creation

COLOSSIANS 3:10

And have put on the new man, which is renewed in knowledge after the image of him that created him

First of all, the church is the new creation. Paul declares that Jesus is the Author of the created world (Col. 1:15–17). Everything was made by Him and through Him and for Him. He sustains creation by His own power and holds everything together. Like a firstborn son in the ancient world who has the rights and privileges over his Father's inheritance, Jesus has first place (preeminence) over all creation. He is also the Head over the new creation, the church (1:18). This is a society of men and women who have been supernaturally created through the regeneration of the Holy Spirit.

The new creation is the result of Christ's deliverance from the fall of Adam. In the Garden of Eden, Adam lived before God in a state of righteousness. However, he acted in disobedience, and the result of his sin was disastrous. His entire nature was transformed. He became a self-centered individual instead of being God-centered. His sin also affected the entire human race. All men now bear the nature of Adam—sinfully depraved and spiritually separated from God. This change has transformed the way we as humans relate to one another. Human society is deeply divided in many ways: language, culture, geography, tradition, and religion. Christ, as the second Adam, came to reverse the curse caused by Adam and to create a new society of people. The walls that separated humanity have now been broken down through Christ. God has created a body in which all believers enter and become a part, regardless of one's background. Christ is all that matters now!

> **WHEN JESUS BECOMES EVERYTHING TO EVERYONE, THERE IS THE POTENTIAL OF INCREDIBLE UNITY IN THE MIDST OF EXTREME DIVERSITY.**

When Jesus becomes everything to everyone, there is the potential of incredible unity in the midst of extreme diversity. His love binds together believers who naturally would hate each other. As the old life with all its prejudices and sin is put off, believers are being united through continual spiritual renewal in the knowledge of Christ. We are a new creation living new lives for a new Master.

Review the categories Paul mentions in Colossians 3:11: Greek (uncircumcised), Jew (circumcised), barbarian (uncultured compared to a Greek), Scythian (an extreme barbarian), bond (slave), and freeman. Discuss some of the natural points of disagreement in a church comprised of such people.

_____

_____

_____

_____

How does a proper view of Christ lead to unity among believers, even with the presence of diversity? For help, consider Philippians 2:1–8.

_____

_____

_____

_____

_____

The New Israel

COLOSSIANS 3:12

Put on therefore, as the elect of God, holy and beloved, bowels of mercies, kindness, humbleness of mind, meekness, longsuffering.

Secondly, the church bears the marks of the new Israel. God chose Israel and made them His treasured possession. They were not chosen because of any special quality they possessed but simply because God decided to love them (Deut. 7:7–8). Now, these same titles are given to the church through Christ. We are *elect*, *holy*, and *beloved*. Believers have been chosen on the basis of God's sovereign will (Eph. 1:4–5).

The attribute *holy* means that the Lord consecrates us. He sets us apart for Himself and His service (Eph. 2:10). Like the nation of Israel, the church is called to reveal by their obedience the character of God and to fulfill His purposes on the earth.

But as he which hath called you is holy, so be ye holy in all manner of conversation (1 Pet. 1:15).

> But ye are a chosen generation, a royal priesthood, an holy nation, a peculiar people; that ye should shew forth the praises of him who hath called you out of darkness into his marvellous light (1 Pet. 2:9).

With the designation *beloved*, Paul reminds us that God has set His love upon us before we chose to love Him (1 John 4:19).

Therefore, the virtues that Paul commands us to put on have everything to do with who we are: a new creation and the new Israel. This is crucial to understand. So often among Christians, character development takes on a self-centered orientation. We pursue it for our own benefit and self-improvement. This was not the way Paul was thinking. He saw these qualities as the way in which the church can give the world a glimpse of the image of God. These were the exact same qualities reflected by God in His relationship with Israel.

WORD STUDY

bowels of mercies—a deep, heartfelt compassion

kindness—displaying gracious acts of kindness for the good of others

humbleness of mind—thinking of others above yourself; not looking to your own interests; serving the needs and interests of others

meekness—not being consumed with one's self-importance; not rebellious or reactionary, but gentle, mild, and patient

longsuffering—enduring mistreatment and faithfully loving others

These are the moral characteristics that believers need in order to act towards others as God has acted towards us. Therefore, Paul commands the Colossians to put on God-like qualities as the church for His name's sake. So when we talk about putting off and putting on and showing love and shunning sin, we cannot think in terms of requirements to pacify some autocratic God or other people. What should be happening is the sometimes slow but sure transformation of sinners into the new man, the image of Christ Himself.

What are some examples of character development in the life of a believer that could have a self-centered emphasis?

_____

_____

_____

_____

_____

The New Way of Life

COLOSSIANS 3:13
Forbearing one another, and forgiving one another, if any man have a quarrel against any: even as Christ forgave you, so also do ye.

WORD STUDY

forbearing—suffering, enduring, or bearing with; putting up with

forgiving—doing a favor; giving freely and graciously; pardoning

quarrel—a legitimate complaint against anyone

bond—that which binds or bands together

perfectness—completeness; perfect harmonizing of the diverse parts

As we noted earlier in this study, God expects us to live out our identity—to become who we are in Christ. In Colossians 3:13 Paul presents two evidences that we are acting like the church and putting Christlike virtue into action: "forbearing one another, and forgiving one another."

The first evidence, *forbearance*, means that we will hold back when provoked and pressured. The present tense of this word tells us that this patience is ongoing and mutual—"for one another." It is enduring.

Forbearance is different than a worldly tolerance that accepts everyone's ideas and lifestyles as equally valid. Mutual forbearance is God's people pursuing the same goal of spreading Christ's fame—so I desire and choose to be patient, not for my advantage, but for Christ's.

Forbearance progresses toward the second evidence, *forgiveness*. There will be times when we have a quarrel or a complaint against another. It is bound to happen, even in a community of believers. The issue Paul is addressing is not the avoidance of friction at all costs. That is impossible in a fallen world. The key is what we do about it. This is not the typical word for forgiveness, but one that especially emphasizes its gracious character. In fact, it comes from the same root as the word *grace*.

Forgiveness does not give up on justice. The unbelief of Jerusalem and its leaders grieved and righteously angered Jesus. Forgiveness does not mean blindly walking into vulnerable situations just because love covers a multitude of sins. God has not given a pass to that person who ridiculed you or mistreated you.

Nevertheless, forgiveness is crucial to Christian relationships. Paul underscores this point by appealing to the pattern of Christ. He could have said, as the New Testament does in other places, that we should forgive others their debts *because* God has forgiven us immeasurably greater debts. But here the

Holy Spirit breathes out the words *even as.* We must forgive just like Christ has forgiven. So how did Christ forgive us? We were his enemies, but He took initiative to grant us forgiveness by overcoming evil with good (Rom. 12:21) and canceling our sin debt (Col. 2:14).

FORBEARANCE AND FORGIVENESS ARE TANGIBLE EXPRESSIONS THAT CHRIST IS OUR LIFE.

We cannot forgive someone's sins against God, but we can choose not to try to make them pay. And if we believe the debt has been paid, we cannot use it as collateral for our present sin. Past wrongs may have led us down a road of despair or bitterness or self-focus, but if God for Christ's sake has paid for our sins and theirs, then those wrongs are no excuse for our persisting in sinful patterns. Christ was not satisfied with neutralizing sinners' evil. He reconciled us to Himself by sacrificing Himself (1:22). He restored the most fractured of relationships. Therefore, it is the true nature of the church to do the same. Forbearance and forgiveness are tangible expressions that Christ is our life.

Forgiveness of our sins is central to our salvation. It is crucial for our relationships, especially as the church. But it can be very difficult. What other Scripture passages provide motivation and direction in this area of forgiveness?

_____   _____

_____

_____

_____

_____

What does it mean to live for something bigger than yourself, and what are some evidences that this is transpiring in your life?

_____

_____

_____

_____

Are the characteristics listed in Colossians 3:12 true in your life? Which one(s) stood out as a significant need in your life?

_____

_____

_____

_____

Is there someone with whom you are currently struggling interpersonally? Do you need to ask forgiveness? What truths do you need to meditate on in order to grow in forbearance and forgiveness?

_____

_____

_____

_____

NOTES

08
THE UNITY OF THE CHURCH

COLOSSIANS 3:14–17
And above all these things put on charity, which is the bond of perfectness. And let the peace of God rule in your hearts, to the which also ye are called in one body; and be ye thankful. Let the word of Christ dwell in you richly in all wisdom; teaching and admonishing one another in psalms and hymns and spiritual songs, singing with grace in your hearts to the Lord. And whatsoever ye do in word or deed, do all in the name of the Lord Jesus, giving thanks to God and the Father by him.

The theme of this section is the unity of the church. Miss this, and you miss the main message. Throughout Colossians Paul focuses on the divisive influence of false teachers. They taught the need of an extra spiritual work subsequent to one's salvation to complete what Christ began in a believer's initial conversion. Among other things, this work appears to have involved some special knowledge not received at salvation. Dick Lucas explains their message this way:

> Through this further crisis of faith, the believer leaves the barrenness and wilderness experience, and enters a new land of promise, flowing with milk and honey. After such an experience, fellowship with the local church seems tame and insipid. It becomes necessary to withdraw with like-minded 'spiritual' people for a 'deeper' experience of fellowship. Whatever form this search for 'fullness' took, there could not fail to be within it,

perhaps hardly realized or recognized, an implicit criticism of the credentials of the local congregation.[1]

Inevitably, if even a few Colossian Christians had adopted this false theology, the effect on the unity of their church would have been staggering.

Paul's divinely-directed theology was different. He emphasized our privileged position in being a part of Christ's church. As God's true representative on the earth, the local church has all its needs supplied in Christ. For believers to withdraw from the fellowship of the local church with the idea of trying to gain something richer and better is actually a terrible loss. Therefore, the apostle gives five commands to counteract the effect of these false teachers and to cultivate unity within the church.

Put On Love

COLOSSIANS 3:14

And above all these things put on charity, which is the bond of perfectness.

As we studied in the last chapter, Christians are to patiently treat one another with compassion and forgiveness. The church is a body of saved sinners. New Christians are spiritual babies who have lots of growing pains. (In fact, all Christian have lots of growing pains!) On many occasions believers will have legitimate complaints against one another because of their immaturities and disobedience. However, these are the situations that God uses to develop true biblical love and the

---

[1]R. C. Lucas, *The Message of Colossians and Philippians* (Downers Grove: InterVarsity Press, 1980), 152.

God-like qualities of compassion, kindness, humility, meekness, and patience. Believers need the church to help bring them to spiritual maturity.

LOVE IS THE CROWNING CHRISTIAN VIRTUE.

Paul concludes in Colossians 3:14 that love holds everything together in perfect harmony like a belt. Love is the crowning Christian virtue. Paul seems to imply that there are those who want to break away from the church in order to have a deeper spiritual experience with a more spiritually elite group. The reality is that they are missing the opportunity to be perfected by learning to love an imperfect body. Shortly before his death Christ declared, "By this shall all men know that ye are my disciples, if ye have love one to another" (John 13:35). Christians should remain in their local churches and humbly accept the multiple opportunities to mature by learning to love different believers from diverse backgrounds. Only through love can a local church develop greater unity.

> *How does love foster a greater unity in the church? What does this look like practically with a diverse group of people? For reference, see how Paul describes such interaction in Romans 12:9–21.*

Let Peace Rule

COLOSSIANS 3:15

And let the peace of God rule in your hearts, to the which also ye are called in one body; and be ye thankful.

WORD STUDY

rule—be an umpire; decide; direct or control

Second, God's peace is to rule and preside over the church, Christ's "one body" (3:15). This verse is often used as a proof text by those who are trying to determine God's will. The idea is that God subjectively directs a believer's life through an experience of inward peace. There is no doubt that God does give His peace to His children (Rom. 5:1; Phil. 4:6–7). However, Paul's point in this text is that believers must make peace a priority in the church. The word *rule* indicates that peace should be the umpire, the deciding factor in our relationships with each other.

This command is rooted in the objective peace Christ has already achieved. He paid the price of His own blood to secure universal *shalom* (i.e., completeness, wholeness, wellness) by reconciling heaven and earth with their Maker (Col. 1:20). We see the significance of this peace when we consider the world of pain, violence, and evil all around us and the guilt and fear within us. So thanks be to God who has "forgiven [us] all trespasses" (2:13) and reconciled us "that were sometime alienated and enemies . . . by wicked works" (1:21). The reality of our peace with God provides the basis of our unity with one another.

Christ is the Head of the church and reigns over a kingdom of peace (Isa. 9:6); therefore, it would be wrong for Christians who have been reconciled to God to be living with unreconciled relationships and unresolved conflicts within the body. Peace should preside over the church's fellowship and rule against any attempt to destroy the church's unity. The church is equipped to be an outpost of God's peace, pointing ahead to the time when *shalom* will fill the entire earth.

> *In His Sermon on the Mount, Jesus calls "peacemakers . . . the children of God" (Matt. 5:9). Why is peacemaking so difficult? Why is it so important? How does it identify someone as a child of God?*

_____

_____

_____

_____

Make the Word at Home

COLOSSIANS 3:16

Let the word of Christ dwell in you richly in all wisdom; teaching and admonishing one another in psalms and hymns and spiritual songs, singing with grace in your hearts to the Lord.

WORD STUDY

dwell—to inhabit; to dwell in one and influence for good

richly—abundantly; copiously

teaching—holding a discourse with others in order to instruct them; imparting instruction; instilling doctrine

admonishing—warning; exhorting

psalms—striking the chords of a musical instrument

hymn—a song of praise

songs—an ode or a song that is spiritual in nature

Third, the Word of Christ is to be the central focus of the church. Is this the word revealed *by* Christ or the word revealed *about* Christ? Probably both. Jesus is both author and subject of divine revelation (Heb. 1:2). God breathed out all of Scripture that His church may be "throughly furnished unto all good works" (2 Tim. 3:17). It is all profitable, and it all points to Christ (John 5:39). His life, His mission, His death and resurrection, His reign, and His will are the foundation of the church (1 Tim. 3:16).

Paul exhorts us to make this message centered on Christ feel at home. God's people, both individually and collectively, must give the word of Christ ample room and free reign in the homes of our hearts. To "dwell . . . richly" does not convey the idea of hosting a guest only in certain rooms because we are embarrassed by the mess everywhere else! The revelation of Jesus Christ must inhabit every square inch of our lives.

How does this take place in the life of a church? Pastors are to enrich the congregation with an abundant supply of Christ-centered Bible exposition. Charles Spurgeon, the "Prince of Preachers," stated it so succinctly: "Let your sermons be full of Christ—from beginning to end crammed full of the Gospel."[2] Preaching Christ is totally sufficient for the spiritual growth of the church. Paul has given us an example of this Christ-exalting approach in the first two chapters of Colossians. As the Word of Christ is preeminent in the ministry of the

---

[2]C. H. Spurgeon, *Soulwinner* (New Kensington, PA: Whitaker House, 1995), 99.

church, it becomes a mutual source of joy for the church and the glue that holds the community together. By growing in this knowledge of Christ and being faithfully warned about false teaching, we will develop a spirit of discernment. God's Word enables us to detect teaching that is infiltrating and disrupting the congregation (Col. 2:8).

Instruction and admonition are not the responsibility of a pastor alone, however. We are to enrich one another through Christ-centered congregational singing. Music is a means for the message of Christ to take deeper root in the community. These types of songs include psalms, hymns, and spiritual songs (3:16). It is difficult to be dogmatic as to the exact kinds of songs these include, but it can be said in general that they are songs of Scripture (*psalms*), songs of praise to Christ (*hymns*), and songs of personal experience and testimony (*spiritual songs*). The direction of the congregation's singing is towards "one another" and "to the Lord." This makes singing both prophecy and worship. Music becomes a form of prophetic communication when believers are engaged in singing truth to one another. "Nothing else teaches and admonishes others as well as the heartfelt, enthusiastic singing that comes from those who know personally what grace means."[3] Music becomes a form of worship when the singing is a heartfelt expression of adoration and gratitude for the grace of Christ. Through both avenues, speaking and singing, oneness in Christ is cultivated in the community.

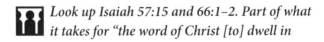 *Look up Isaiah 57:15 and 66:1–2. Part of what it takes for "the word of Christ [to] dwell in*

---

[32]Richard R. Melick Jr., *The New American Commentary: Philippians, Colossians, Philemon* (Nashville: Broadman and Holman Publishers, 1991), 306.

you richly" is a humble response to preaching. What
gets in the way of our consistently responding in this
way to the preached Word?

Do Everything for Christ

COLOSSIANS 3:17

And whatsoever ye do in word or deed, do all in the
name of the Lord Jesus, giving thanks to God and
the Father by him.

Fourth, the name of Christ is what compels the church. Perhaps
it seems like it could go without saying that we should do everything for Christ's sake. But Paul does not leave this fundamental
command unstated. Nor does he couch it in tentative language
but instead uses comprehensive terms, *whatsoever* and *all*. "The
name of the Lord Jesus" is to be our all-consuming motivation.
By our speech and our actions we must show that He is our
Lord. He opened the way to the Father with His own blood. *In
Jesus' name* is not just a prayer hashtag. It is the Christian life.

Keep Giving Thanks

COLOSSIANS 3:17

Giving thanks to God and the Father by him.

There is one more facet of these verses we should note. It is
clear that we must keep our focus on Christ and that when we
do, the church will enjoy unity. But how is this possible? At

the conclusion of three consecutive verses Paul urges believers to express gratefulness: "and be ye thankful . . . singing with [gratitude] in your hearts to the Lord . . . giving thanks to God and the Father by him" (3:15–17). Spiritual unity is maintained through a continually thankful heart.

Paul's theology can be summed up as *grace*, and His ethics as *gratitude*. Gratitude is the only fitting response to God's grace. What we deserve is eternal death, but we have received the exact opposite. Therefore, gratitude should be our default and touch every contour of our lives—relationships, worship, and work. Being thankful for the church itself elevates its importance in our hearts and minds. Being thankful protects us from a complaining spirit. Being thankful nurtures a humble spirit. Those who are full of gratitude find it easier to extend the grace of love and forgiveness to fellow believers and put aside petty issues that might inhibit the expression of peace in the community.

WE MUST LET CHRIST'S PEACE RULE AMONG US.

Christian unity is vitally important. In fact, one way the world knows that the Father sent His Son to be our Savior is that believers are "one, even as we [the Trinity] are one" (John 17:22). Therefore, life in Christ is life together as His body. Paul's commands in Colossians 3:14–17 are no small matter. We must put on love as the belt that brings Christian virtue together. We must let Christ's peace rule among us. We must make the word of Christ the true homeowner of our hearts. We must do everything in His name. And we have more than enough reason to continually give thanks.

Describe the importance of thankfulness and graciousness among believers. How could your group encourage one another to live gratefully?

_____

_____

_____

_____

Have you ever experienced disunity in your local church? Which one(s) of the five commands in this study would have made a significant difference in that situation?

_____

_____

_____

_____

Look up Isaiah 53:5. Meditate on what Christ did to achieve peace. Use this meditation in prayer concerning your own relationships.

_____

_____

_____

_____

Did "the word of Christ dwell in you richly" this past week? How about the past month? Are there changes you need to make in your daily schedule to make this a priority?

_____

_____

_____

_____

_____

NOTES

09
PLEASING CHRIST AT HOME

COLOSSIANS 3:18–21
Wives, submit yourselves unto your own husbands, as it is fit in the Lord. Husbands, love your wives, and be not bitter against them. Children, obey your parents in all things: for this is well pleasing unto the Lord. Fathers, provoke not your children to anger, lest they be discouraged.

You cannot purchase a home (new or old) without understanding that being a homeowner requires constant maintenance and upkeep. Fixing and improving a home is the consistent responsibility of its owner. This is also true when you establish a home through marriage and a family through having or adopting children. It entails an ongoing process of improvement.

Though the church becomes a spiritual family for believers, it does not replace God's design for a stable home—husband and wife, parents and children. In Colossians 3:18–21, Paul addresses the members of a Christian home with regards to his or her role and responsibilities in the home. After reading these verses, a few questions should come to mind.

First, are these commands sufficient for building a Christian home? They are so short and simple, even abrupt. Is there not more to the family than what has been written?

Second, does a Christian view of the family negate the equality of individuals? It may appear from these verses that the wife and the child are put in a place of inferiority, even vulnerability.

Third, do these commands create a cultural conflict? The idea of a wife being submissive could create tension. Should these roles and responsibilities not be altered or adjusted because of the culture? Does the definition of a biblical family conflict with those who are proponents of a non-traditional family, such as family built on a same-sex union?

Fourth, who is ultimately responsible for the family? The way we view the family must be seen through the lenses of salvation. We are members of the family of God and are called new creations ("the new man") in Christ (Col. 3:10).

> IF OUR FAITH IS TO BE GENUINE, IT WILL TOUCH EVERY REALM OF OUR LIVES, INCLUDING OUR OWN HUMAN FAMILIES.

As members of this family of believers, we are commanded to live out our new identity in every area of our life under the complete lordship of Christ. If our faith is to be genuine, it will touch every realm of our lives, including our own human families. These commands therefore reveal how a Christian family is to look and operate under the authority of Jesus Christ.

Paul's pattern is to speak directly to each family member (wives, husbands, children, fathers), to give each one his or her divine responsibility, and then to give a motivating reason behind the command.

Wives

COLOSSIANS 3: 18

Wives, submit yourselves unto your own husbands,
as it is fit in the Lord.

To submit means "to place oneself under" or "to subject one-self." In military terms it involves *rank*. In relation to government this term denotes citizens who are *obedient*. It is very clear that Paul's approach is to address first the one who is placed in a subordinate role.

In an age where individual rights are prominent, particularly in a country such as the United States, this command may seem to demean women. In fact, it has been interpreted as a contradiction to what Paul has said in other places, even a few verses earlier in Colossians 3, about the equality of all believers.

> There is neither Jew nor Greek, there is neither bond nor free, there is neither male nor female: for ye are all one in Christ Jesus (Gal. 3:28).

> Where there is neither Greek nor Jew, circumcision nor uncircumcision, Barbarian, Scythian, bond nor free: but Christ is all, and in all (Col. 3:11).

It is very clear that Paul places no distinction between men and women in their relationship with God. We are all equally one. This is not surprising, because He explicitly created the first man and woman (Adam and Eve) equally in His own image (Gen. 1:27). Therefore, submission has nothing to do with competence or value.

But if we are equal image-bearers and equal members of Christ's body, why should wives submit to husbands? It is all about the way the family is to function! Consider three truths.

God Has Established a Functional Order.

Relationships in the home are rooted in the Trinity. The Father, the Son, and the Holy Spirit are co-equal with one another. However, there is a functional order in the Trinity where one person of the Godhead submits Himself to another person in order to accomplish God's sovereign purposes.

For example, Jesus totally submitted Himself to His Father's will. Why? In order to accomplish the Father's plan and purpose of our redemption. Likewise, the Holy Spirit functions in submission to the Father's sovereign will by working in the hearts of those whom the Father has chosen to be heirs of salvation. So within the Trinity equality and submission co-exist, and this submission has a functional purpose in our salvation.

God has also revealed a functional order in the family:

> But I would have you know, that the head of every man is Christ; and the head of the woman is the man; and the head of Christ is God (1 Cor. 11:3).

In order for the family to function there is a divine flowchart, an order of responsibility and accountability. The duties of the subordinate are always first, because if there is no submission everything will fall apart. Just like in the Trinity, there is equality between husbands and wives, but submission is necessary for the family to function. They are equal in essence but complementarily different in function.

This Submission Is Always Voluntary.

The grammar of Paul's command indicates this is a voluntary submission. By way of contrast, Paul states his command that children obey with a stronger form that does not emphasize volunteerism. God's ideal is not that a wife comes kicking and screaming but rather joyfully and willingly submits to her husband. Role differences do not translate into superiority or inferiority. They are both equal. In fact, the trajectory Paul is setting is that both the husband and the wife share in mutual responsibilities. The husband is commanded to obey God by loving his wife and making her needs, desires, and wishes his focus.

This Submission Is Ultimately to the Lord.

Paul says it is "fit" or proper for the wife to submit to her husband "in the Lord." In other words, the motivation is not a man's dominance but rather Christ's preeminence. He is the Head of the church of which we are a part (Eph. 5:24). Submission in the home is defined by God, not culture. Therefore, biblical submission does not ask a wife to disobey God by obeying her husband. Such obedience would not be fitting, for all of us are ultimately under the authority of our Lord.

*Read Romans 13:1 and 1 Peter 5:5. Discuss how the idea of **submission** in these two passages compares to Colossians 3:18.*

_____

_____

_____

_____

How does Jesus Christ's relationship to His Father help us understand a wife's role in marriage?

_____

_____

_____

_____

Husbands

COLOSSIANS 3:19

Husbands, love your wives, and be not bitter against them.

Paul gives husbands two commands. The first is positive. Husbands must love their wives. This was an unusual command in ancient times. The widespread notion among Greeks and Jews was that wives were to submit; however, there was no reciprocal code in the ancient world requiring husbands to love their wives. The second command is negative. Husbands must not be harsh with their wives. This love is distinctly sacrificial—a self-giving love modeled by Christ. It means considering a wife's every need and showing her the greatest respect.

The fall did not cause gender roles in marriage; it perverted them. Since we all sinned in Adam, wives are tempted to control their husbands, and husbands are tempted either to abdicate their responsibility or use it in manipulative and unloving ways. With frightening regularity, a husband destroys this closest and dearest of relationships because his wife fails to live up to his ideals, his hopes, and his ambitions—physically, mentally, emotionally, financially, relationally.

Ironically, everything a husband thinks his wife needs to change in her life is a reflection of what he needs to change in his own. A wife is simply a mirror reflection of her husband. Husbands love wives, not by controlling them but by serving them. The lordship of Christ demands that we love!

Read Ephesians 5:25–30 and 1 Peter 3:7. What do these passages teach about loving male leadership?

_____

_____

_____

_____

_____

** 👥 *What about before marriage? Are there
principles for how young men should treat
young women to whom they are not married? Read 1
Timothy 5:2. What implications does this verse have
for a dating relationship? What implications does it
have for the lines of authority in a young woman's life
before she is married?***

_____

_____

_____

_____

Children

COLOSSIANS 3:20

Children, obey your parents in all things: for this is
well pleasing unto the Lord.

Children are also addressed as responsible persons within
the congregation. The responsibilities within the family are
mutual; even children have a role. The root of the word *obey*
means to listen. Consider Deuteronomy 6:4: "Hear, O Israel:
The Lord our God is one Lord." In this context, listening and
obeying are virtually synonymous. It is an eager ear that listens
with the intent to obey absolutely.

Paul seems to be addressing children who are living under the
protection and care of their parents. They are obligated to obey

in all aspects of life, including time and schedule, friends, entertainment, and dress. This is appropriate behavior within the Christian community.

Children who do not live at home should show deference but are no longer expected to obey. However, the command to "honour thy father and mother" has no statute of limitations (Eph. 6:2). Furthermore, the motivation remains the same. In relation to our parents, we must do what is "well pleasing to the Lord."

Write down five ways that college students who still live at home should apply Colossians 3:20 and Ephesians 6:1–2.

_____

_____

_____

_____

_____

Fathers

COLOSSIANS 3:21
Fathers, provoke not your children to anger, lest they be discouraged.

By divine intention, the father is primarily responsible for motivating his children. It is easy to provoke children so that they become disheartened. This exasperation sucks the life out of their passion to please their parents.

Children naturally want to bring their parents pleasure. Every father of young children knows the delighted plea, "Daddy, watch me!" I remember looking toward the stands as a football player hoping to see my parents sitting there. I remember as a freshman in college sitting on the bench as we played Erskine College and looking up and seeing my father, who drove 92 miles to come to the game. I remember how encouraged I was to have my father attend my college graduation. I also remember how my father, who was paralyzed from his chest down, said to me one week before he died how proud he was of me.

No Christian father inherently desires to dishearten his children, but it happens regularly. How? Dads say and do things in ways that contradicts their acceptance of their children. Their love and approval is, or at least seems, conditional. This happens through anger and abuse as well as apathy and absence. It might be nagging, belittling, or criticism. It might be the repeated failure to acknowledge worthy achievements.

We see the effects in children who are unusually fearful, withdrawn, and so timid that they lack normal self-confidence. They start believing they have amounted to nothing. The overbearing emotional strength of a father can crush his children. His irritability can beat them down. A father should admonish his children, correcting wrong attitudes and wrong behavior. However, he must also constantly nurture them through good counsel and encouraging words.

In this passage Paul does not directly address single adults living on their own, though he characterizes singlehood positively elsewhere (1 Cor. 7:32–35). What truths from Colossians 3:18–21 should single adults apply to their circumstances?

Conclusion

Let's return to our initial questions. First, are these commands sufficient? They are, because they provide a framework to demonstrate resurrected life in a family context. Furthermore, specific commands in this paragraph of Paul's letter regarding relationships are rooted in the general commands in the preceding paragraphs. Second, does Christian teaching about the family undermine the equality of the individual? Absolutely not! Paul's inspired words actually elevate the individual by giving him or her purpose and meaning in fulfilling roles and responsibilities. Third, is there a cultural conflict with these commands? Increasingly, yes. The roles and responsibilities within a family vary somewhat among cultures. However, the fundamental laws of the family are unalterable. The biblical definition of a family conflicts with the current belief of many in our society. That can greatly intimidate us, but we should embrace our contemporary context as an opportunity to shine the gospel light brightly through counter-cultural, God-honoring family relationships. Finally, who is responsible for the family? Everyone! A family works well only when each person takes responsibility for his or her divinely created role.

THE SINS THAT DESTROY THE FABRIC OF CHRISTIAN COMMUNITIES START BY DISINTEGRATING THE THREADS OF CHRISTIAN FAMILIES.

The sins that destroy the fabric of Christian communities start by disintegrating the threads of Christian families: bad morality, bad communication, pride, lack of forgiveness, disunity, and more. Instead, we must be vigilant as family members, heeding Paul's admonition: "As ye have therefore received Christ Jesus the Lord, so walk ye in Him" (Col. 2:6).

What aspect of these four verses caused you to think the most? Why?

_____

_____

_____

_____

_____

Perhaps your own family background is somewhat (or very) troubled. What are some comforting truths from Colossians 3 that you can apply when thinking about your family—past and future?

_____

_____

_____

_____

_____

NOTES

10
CHRIST IS LORD AT WORK

COLOSSIANS 3:22–4:1

Servants, obey in all things your masters according to the flesh;
not with eyeservice, as menpleasers; but in singleness of heart,
fearing God: and whatsoever ye do, do it heartily, as to the Lord,
and not unto men; knowing that of the Lord ye shall receive
the reward of the inheritance: for ye serve the Lord Christ. But
he that doeth wrong shall receive for the wrong which he hath
done: and there is no respect of persons. Masters, give unto
your servants that which is just and equal; knowing that ye also
have a Master in heaven.

Work has existed since the beginning of time. In fact, God was the original worker, though His work of breathing creation into existence in six days was seemingly effortless. The difficulty of labor came with the Fall. That is why work on this fallen planet is ultimately dissatisfying. Ecclesiastes teaches that we can enjoy it, but there will be a sense of futility at times, and certainly pain and difficulty. But though we still feel the effects of the Fall, we now work in the present in light of redemption. We work as unto the Lord. It matters whether we bring God glory in our work, just like it matters whether we meditate on God's Word. In fact, the latter must lead to the former. In his application of new life in Christ, Paul addresses this very important issue of our work.

The Issue of Slavery

COLOSSIANS 3:22 & 4:1

Servants, obey in all things your masters according
to the flesh; . . . Masters, give unto your servants that

which is just and equal; knowing that ye also have
a Master in heaven.

The fact that Paul addresses *servants* (3:22) and *masters* (4:1)
introduces the issue of slavery. Unfortunately, some segments
of the Christian church have been very wrong about slavery.
For example, there were Christian advocates of slavery in the
United States prior to, during, and even after the Civil War.
Thankfully, there have also been standout opponents to slavery, such as William Wilberforce. He waged a twenty-year
battle in British Parliament against the slave trade that ended
in its being outlawed in 1807. Then, just three days before
Wilberforce died, Parliament abolished slavery itself in most
of the British Empire in 1833. Greatly influenced and encouraged by John Newton, Wilberforce charted a bold, biblical
path forward as a result of his evangelical beliefs.

But slavery is not just a historical phenomenon. The modern-
day manifestations of it are often grouped together under the
heading *human trafficking*. It is a fast-growing criminal industry in many parts of our world. Human trafficking includes,
for example, the commercial sex trade that destroys adults and
children alike. There is no doubt about the wickedness of this
industry. God clearly condemns "menstealers" (1 Tim. 1:10).

RACIAL PREJUDICE
HAS NO PLACE IN THE
CHURCH EITHER BECAUSE
GOD HAS RECONCILED
ETHNICITIES INTO ONE
BODY.

Unlike marriage (Gen
2:24) and male leader-
ship in local churches
(1 Tim 2:11–14), slav-
ery is not grounded in
Creation but in the Fall.
That is why a person's
status in the church is
Christian, not slave or
free (Col 3:11). Racial
prejudice has no place in the church either because God has
reconciled ethnicities into one body (Eph. 2:13–16). Racism

certainly does not exist around the throne of God above, where saints from "every kindred, and tongue, and people, and nation" are gathering to worship the Lamb who was slain to redeem them to His Father (Rev 5:9).

When we read Paul's words to slaves and masters in Colossians, we need to realize that slavery was an integral part of the Roman Empire in the first century. Perhaps one-third of the people in Colossae were slaves. Although it may seem counterintuitive, a radical push for liberation would probably have meant great risk for them personally. Furthermore, Christians were a small group without social significance who viewed their calling as cultivating a new reality in the midst of the still existing old one. As one commentator puts it, "The issue was not that of the acceptance of an institution sanctioned by law and part of the fabric of Graeco-Roman civilization; nor was it a question of how to react to a demand for its abolition . . . Rather, it concerned the tension between the freedom given in Christ (cf. 3:11) and the 'slavery' in which Christian slaves are to continue to serve their earthly masters."[1]

In fact, Paul's teaching pointed to the termination of slavery. Paul sent this letter to the Colossians in the hands of two men, Tychicus and Onesimus (Col. 4:7, 9). The latter was a slave of Philemon who had run away to Rome, perhaps after robbing Philemon (Philemon 1:18). When Paul wrote the Colossians, he also wrote Philemon appealing that he should receive Onesimus back as a brother in Christ.

> For perhaps [Onesimus] therefore departed for a season, that thou shouldest receive him forever; not now as a servant, but above a servant, a brother beloved, specially to me, but how much more unto

[1]O'Brien, 226.

thee, both in the flesh, and in the Lord? (Philem. 1:15–16)

In other words, while Paul's agenda in Colossians is clearly not a social revolution, the apostle does lay the groundwork for abolition by his strong appeal on behalf of Onesimus.

Though most of us have had no personal experience with slavery, there is plenty of application in these verses for us. Work is an integral part of our everyday lives, and usually we are a boss, an employee managed by a boss, or both. If our new life in Christ is supposed to shape how we live now, we must consider our jobs. In this passage the Holy Spirit confronts us with this question: Who is my lord when it comes to labor? Paul uses the title *Kurios* throughout this letter to refer to Jesus Christ, including five times in this section (Col. 3:22–4:1). His point is that regardless of whether you are slave or master, entry-level laborer or millionaire, Jesus is the Lord of your labor.

Mandates to Serve

COLOSSIANS 3:22

Servants, obey in all things your masters according to the flesh.

It is noteworthy that the section addressing slaves is four times as long as the one to masters. There are probably two reasons for this. First, the Colossian church's demographic was undoubtedly weighted heavily toward slaves, not masters. It makes sense that Paul would focus more application on them. In addition, because Onesimus accompanied Tychicus with this letter, Onesimus's relationship with Philemon would have been a point of interest for the Colossian church. They probably wondered what counsel Paul had for them, since he had taken a particular interest in Onesimus's situation.

SEEKING THINGS ABOVE: A STUDY IN COLOSSIANS

There are two inseparable commands (3:22, 23) in these four verses of instruction to subordinates. In verse 22 Paul tells servants to "obey." This is the exact same word he used two verses earlier to instruct children. There is no question of whether or not a subordinate worker should obey the directives of his or her superior. The exception to this comprehensive command would be when a boss tells his employee to do something sinful. We know this because in verse 24 Paul says "ye serve the Lord Christ," and we cannot do this by sinning.

The second command is to "do *it* heartily, as to the Lord, and not unto men" (3:23). Faithful, hard, honest work honors the Lord, not because of self-effort but because He is our true Master and we live for His pleasure. Therefore, the two-fold command to those working for another is to work with integrity and ultimately to serve the Lord Christ. By comparison, the reality of serving Christ by working faithfully is like the reality of loving Christ by demonstrating love to someone in need. In Christ we can and we must glorify God at work.

Means to Serve

COLOSSIANS 3:22–23

Servants, obey in all things your masters according to the flesh; not with eyeservice, as menpleasers; but in singleness of heart, fearing God: and whatsoever ye do, do it heartily, as to the Lord, and not unto men.

Such sweeping statements may leave us wondering how far this service should go. Doesn't everyone struggle at work sometimes? First, Paul speaks unambiguously concerning the extent of our service. He says, "Servants, obey in all things your masters according to the flesh" (3:22). In other words, whatever your human boss says to do, listen and submit. The following verse is just as comprehensive: "And whatsoever ye do" (3:23). This paragraph of Scripture indicates that our labor is not merely a physical necessity but an opportunity for worship. If we are to glorify God in whatever we do (1 Cor. 10:31), then we must obey our human employer consistently.

Second, Paul speaks emphatically about the manner of our service. He uses a picturesque phrase, "not with eyeservice" (Col. 3:22). In other words, we must not work superficially or do just enough to get by. He adds to this the idea of being "menpleasers," which means doing your job only when the boss is looking over your shoulder. However, simply keeping your boss from being suspicious is not the ultimate goal.

In contrast Paul directs us to work "in singleness of heart" (3:22). This singular focus and unwavering concentration enables us to do more than the bare minimum. Instead of begrudgingly trying to be productive enough to ensure a paycheck, having Christ as Lord of our labor means we will serve "heartily" (3:23). This does not mean we bounce off walls with uncontainable excitement. It does convey a wholehearted commitment and integrity that refuses hypocrisy—the disparity between what we know to do and what we actually do. We serve the Lord faithfully and with singular focus.

> *In what ways are you tempted to please people instead of Jesus Christ through your work? What truths from Colossians 3 would renew your mind to change in this area?*

_____

_____

_____

_____

Our society tends to have a live-for-the-weekend mentality. All of us certainly need rest. However, what about this mindset could easily contradict Paul's instruction in Colossians 3?

_____

_____

_____

_____

_____

Motivations to Serve

COLOSSIANS 3:24–25

Knowing that of the Lord ye shall receive the reward of the inheritance: for ye serve the Lord Christ. But he that doeth wrong shall receive for the wrong which he hath done: and there is no respect of persons.

False teachers in Colossae were promoting a Christianity that prided itself in wisdom through spiritual visions and special rules. Apostolic Christianity, however, is focused on eternal life in Christ in such a way that invests our temporal life with true meaning and purpose. In Colossians 3:24–25 God declares not only what we should do and how we should do it but also why.

Reward

COLOSSIANS 3:24

Knowing that of the Lord ye shall receive the reward of the inheritance.

Paul begins in verse 24 with the encouraging prospect of reward. By using the word "knowing" he reminds us of a truth we need to continually bring to mind. Our reward is our inheritance as a fellow heir with Christ. It is "incorruptible, and undefiled, and . . . fadeth not away, [and is] reserved in heaven for you" (1 Pet. 1:4). The Holy Spirit is the down payment and seal of this inheritance (Eph. 1:13). This idea of an inheritance looks back to several previous points in Paul's epistle to the Colossians: 1:5 (hope), 1:12 (saints' inheritance), 1:27 (hope of glory), and 3:1–4 (the things above where Christ your life is).

Regardless of how heartless your employer might be, we serve a gracious Lord. Therefore, we work with reverent awe or "fear" for God (3:22). He bought us with a price (1 Cor. 6:20), freeing us from slavish fear of man. Our participation in the gospel delivers us from bondage to sin and motivates us to serve Christ gratefully, not grudgingly, even at work.

We have a lot of stuff in the twenty-first century, but these Colossian slaves would have immediately recognized the striking paradox of having little hope of temporal inheritance but confident expectation of an unfathomable, eternal inheritance in Christ. So fundamentally, we do not work for a paycheck or a promotion. We work because of a person and His promise.

Recompense

COLOSSIANS 3:25
But he that doeth wrong shall receive for the wrong which he hath done: and there is no respect of persons.

The reminder at the end of Colossians 3:24 leads to a second motivation in 3:25. It may seem strange to warn slaves about doing wrong. What about the fact that they are owned by another person? We are usually drawn to characters like *Robin Hood*, who rob from the rich to give to the poor. But God is not partial: "there is no respect of persons" (3:25). The point is not so much that slaves are disobeying earthly masters but that wrongdoing in such a relationship is ultimately an offence to God. Slaves who do wrong, though disadvantaged from a human standpoint, are held accountable. Our identity in Christ does not give us a pass in the so-called secular areas of life. We will all give an account (2 Cor. 5:10).

How does the affluence of contemporary culture cause difficulty when trying to focus on our heavenly inheritance? What can we do to fix our gaze on eternal reward, instead of temporal? How would this affect what we do at work?

_____

_____

_____

_____

Masters Who Serve

COLOSSIANS 4:1

Masters, give unto your servants that which is just and equal; knowing that ye also have a Master in heaven.

WHEREAS THE UNSAVED WORLD TENDS TO USE PEOPLE AND LOVE STUFF, THOSE OF US WHO HAVE NEW LIFE IN CHRIST MUST LOVE PEOPLE AND USE STUFF.

In Colossians 3:22 Paul speaks of "masters according to the flesh." Though in other places the word *flesh* has a wholly negative connotation, here it simply means *human* or *in this temporal world*. Christians who oversee fellow human beings must take the initiative to "give . . . that which is just and equal" (4:1). Those who serve under you may not have an equal position, and being fellow members of the church does not obliterate those distinctions at work (3:11). However, harsh, repressive policies and practices have no place in a Christian employer's life. Whereas the unsaved world tends to use people and love stuff, those of us who have new life in Christ must love people and use stuff. A Christian who is a manager of fellow human beings is still a servant of Christ. Regardless of our position or status or wealth we "have a Master in heaven" (4:1).

What would it look like for a Christian employer to serve Christ as Lord in his work?

_____

_____

_____

_____

Conclusion

What God requires of us in life is rooted in what He provides for us in Christ. We do not work to earn God's favor. We work in grateful response to His favor. God is not looking for work-aholics, but He does draw pleasure from people who work for His name's sake—who refuse to compartmentalize His saving grace from their jobs.

Paul's ultimate point to the Colossians is that Jesus Christ is to be everything to everyone. He is totally sufficient for every need in the Church.

- The word of Christ is sufficient for our preaching (1:28).

SEEKING THINGS ABOVE: A STUDY IN COLOSSIANS

- The presence of Christ is sufficient for living (1:27; 2:6, 10).

- The power of Christ is sufficient to overcome sin (3:9–10).

- The fellowship we have in Christ is sufficient for our unity (3:11, 15).

- The peace of Christ is sufficient to rule the church (3:15).

- The relationship we have with Christ is sufficient to build our family (3:18–21).

- The lordship of Christ is sufficient to work faithfully (3:22–4:1).

Our response to this sufficiency is to submit continually and joyfully to His preeminence over every area of our new lives in Christ (1:18).

What motivates you to work—whether in the classroom or on the jobsite? What effect(s) should this passage have on your mindset and practice?

_____

_____

_____

_____

Have you been unfaithful or dishonest in one of your jobs? Have you repented of this sin and made it right with your employer?

_____

_____

_____

_____

_____

What has been your experience with Christian employers in the past? Though all of us are sinners, have they sincerely lived out the truth of this passage?

_____

_____

_____

_____

_____

NOTES